Embracing Writing

First- and Second-Year Writing at Bridgewater State University

Sixth Edition

Julia Stakhnevich
Jennifer A. Fallas
Daniel Johnson
Randi M. Rezendes
Shelagh M. Smith
Bridgewater State University

Kendall Hunt publishing company

www.kendallhunt.com
Send all inquiries to:
4050 Westmark Drive
Dubuque, IA 52004-1840

Dedicated with respect and appreciation to the
adjunct faculty of the English Department
at Bridgewater State University

≈ Contents ≈

Contents   **vii**

To the Student

Embracing Writing will be useful to you in several ways as you develop as a writer in BSU's writing program. The goals of the writing program include developing nuanced and meaningful arguments; locating, evaluating, integrating, and documenting primary and secondary sources to support your arguments; focusing and organizing your writing; moving through the processes of writing–inventing, composing, revising, editing, and proofreading–according to the conventions of standard written English; and composing in a voice appropriate to the audience and purpose of your writing.

You may find the following features of this book to be especially helpful:

- **A list of important resources.** These resources include the Writing Studio, where experienced consultants can give you feedback on your work before you turn it in. As a client in the Writing Studio, you may bring in work you have written independently or work you have written for a class–any class, not just an English class. The Writing Studio is a useful resource in helping you fine-tune your work not only before you submit it to your professor, but also before you submit it for publication in one of BSU's many journals. In addition to the Writing Studio, the list of resources includes the counseling center; technological resources, including many that are useful but little known; and the library, which can help you in more ways than you may realize.

- **A list of places you can publish and present your work**. BSU students have important things to say–things that are worthy of reaching a larger audience. In addition, publishing or presenting your work looks good on your résumé and is personally gratifying.

- **A section on helpful strategies for writing**. The strategies described in this section will help you to write even more effectively.

- **Essays written by ENGL 101, ENGL 102, First Year Seminar, and Second Year Seminar students**. In addition to being interesting reading, each essay features an introduction that discusses the rhetorical strategies used by the writer–strategies that you may want to use in your own writing. Having these illustrations at your disposal may help you produce even better work.

- **The submission and award information that you'll need when you submit your work for consideration in next year's *Embracing Writing*. The book publishes student writing in Writing I, Writing II, First Year Seminar, and Second Year Seminar.**

Awards are given for excellence in the following categories in Writing I and Writing II: Persuasive Writing, Creative Non-Fiction, and Researched Writing. Additional awards for 2012 include Excellence in First Year Seminar Writing, Excellence in Second Year Seminar Writing, Excellence in Writing on the Topic of Sustainability, and Excellence in Writing Quantitative Argument. The first place winner in each category receives $50 and guaranteed publication in the next edition of *Embracing Writing*. For more information about the submission process, please see the last page in this book. If you have any questions, contact Dr. Julia Stakhnevich (jstakhnevich@bridgew.edu).

Mission Statement of the First-Year Writing Program at BSU

The mission of the first-year writing program at Bridgewater State University is to teach students the conventions of writing in the college classroom and to demonstrate the importance of critical reading and writing beyond the classroom as students enter into communities and become responsible, concerned citizens. Because the work students undertake in both ENGL 101 and ENGL 102 is important to nearly all other classes they will take at Bridgewater State University, it makes sense that both courses are taken in the first year. In addition to ENGL 101 and ENGL 102, students are required to take a First Year Seminar and Second Year Seminar, which, like ENGL 101 and ENGL 102, focus on the development of college-level writing skills.

All of the writing that students do is undertaken against a backdrop of a classroom alive with texts: texts that students create and texts of published writers. Reading has a central role in first-year writing classes. A substantial part of ENGL 101 is devoted to helping students become better readers of their own writing as well as the writing of others. Conversations about writing, reading, and literacy focus on the rhetorical effects of argument on readers and writers as people in the world.

The balance between preparing students for college-level writing and developing critical literacy among new college writers is the constant concern of faculty teaching the courses. Each class works differently to reflect that balance in the nature and number of writing assignments presented in the classroom, but all of them reflect particular shared outcomes for each course.

Learning Outcomes for First-Year Writing Courses, FYS, and SYS

Though each section of these courses will vary in content, readings, and projects, each section is designed to meet the following learning objectives. As you will notice from reading through these objectives, the learning objectives for First Year Seminar (FYS) are meant to be complementary to those in ENGL 101 and ENGL 102, and the learning objectives in Second Year Seminar (SYS) build on all three of these courses.

ENGL 101: Writing Rhetorically

In this course, students will:

- Develop rhetorical awareness by understanding how to analyze the purpose and audience for specific writing situations and use this analysis to guide their writing and reading.
- Formulate a focused, arguable thesis and support this thesis in an effectively organized essay with evidence drawn from class readings, class discussions, and their knowledge and experience.
- Approach writing as a recursive process which involves inventing, composing, revising, and editing.
- Compose in a voice appropriate for the genre, goals, and target audience.
- Critically read and respond to a variety of texts, including published texts, their peers' texts, and their own texts.
- Use technology to write, revise, and deliver documents.
- Demonstrate facility in using the conventions of Standard Written English, including the conventions of sentence structure, usage, and punctuation.

ENGL 102: Writing Rhetorically with Sources

In this course, students will:

- Continue to grow as a writer and reader in relation to the ENGL 101 outcomes.
- Become familiar with conducting research through the use of electronic academic research tools, such as Maxwell Library's online catalogue and electronic research databases.

- Locate both primary and secondary source materials and evaluate their credibility.
- Approach research as a recursive process, consisting of a series of tentative hypotheses that are then tested and affirmed or revised.
- Effectively integrate secondary sources into their own text, using an appropriate citation style, while demonstrating a clear awareness of the relationship of these sources to the writer's central point and a clear distinction between the ideas and language of the writer and those of the sources.

First Year Seminar Outcomes

If a First Year Seminar satisfies a distribution area, then it must address the outcomes of knowing and understanding the intellectual foundations, conceptual frameworks, and methodologies of that distribution area. In addition, FYS students will:

- Using best practices, develop fluency in written expression; craft coherent paragraphs; use prose that is clear, correct, concise, and varied; use standard academic English.
- Read a wide range of materials purposefully, with comprehension and skill in critical inquiry.
- Be able to work collaboratively and independently.
- Gather appropriate background information on a topic related to knowing and understanding the intellectual foundations, conceptual frameworks, and methodologies of the distribution area that the course addresses.
- Make use of basic information literacy and technology and skills covered in ENGL 101 and ENGL 102.

The course must require significant writing. This would be satisfied by three papers, each being a minimum of five pages, or any requirement comparable to this. In addition to the number of pages, the student must be given regular feedback on his/her written work.

Second Year Seminar Outcomes

If a Second Year Seminar satisfies a distribution area, then it must address the outcomes of knowing and understanding the intellectual frameworks, and methodologies of that distribution area. In addition, SYS students will:

- Using best practices, develop fluency in written expression; craft coherent paragraphs; use prose that is clear, correct, concise, and varied; use standard academic English.
- Read a wide range of materials purposefully, with comprehension and skill in critical inquiry.
- Be able to work collaboratively and independently.

- Gather appropriate background information on a topic related to knowing and understanding the intellectual foundations, conceptual frameworks, and methodologies of the distribution area that the course addresses.
- Make use of basic information literacy and technology and skills covered in ENGL 101 and ENGL 102.

If writing intensive, the course must require significant writing. This could be satisfied by three papers, each being a minimum of five pages, or any requirement comparable to this. In addition to the number of pages, the student must be given regular feedback on his/her work. If speaking intensive, the course should have as a goal that the students enhance their abilities to speak clearly, effectively, and confidently in both large and small groups, as when presenting a report, participating on a panel, debating, or articulating judgments and opinions.

Course Descriptions

Below are catalogue descriptions of the writing courses offered as part of the first year writing program at BSU, as well as for First Year Seminar and Second Year Seminar, courses important to the core curriculum. Information about prerequisites and credits for these courses are available online at the *Bridgewater State University/Undergraduate/ Graduate Catalogue*, which is available online <http://www.bridgew.edu/ catalog/>.

In spring 2009, the English department voted to change the name of ENGL 101 from Writing I to Writing Rhetorically, and ENGL 102 from Writing II to Writing Rhetorically with Sources, along with revised learning objectives and course catalogue descriptions, to be effective in spring 2010. The course descriptions below and outcomes in the following section of this book reflect these changes.

ENGL 101: Writing Rhetorically

By intensive practice in composing persuasive texts, writers explore various techniques for discovering, developing, and organizing ideas in relation to rhetorical context. Special attention is given to developing an effective writing process and an awareness of the relationships among text, audience, and purpose.

ENGL 102: Writing Rhetorically with Sources

Continuing to develop knowledge of persuasive writing and rhetoric, the writer learns and practices various approaches to conducting research and to integrating the ideas of others into one's own text. Emphasis is on writing longer and more substantive texts that incorporate a variety of sources.

Targeted Sections of ENGL 101 and 102

There are also four special options of these courses designed for specific groups of students: Targeted 101, Targeted 101 for Language, Targeted 102, and Targeted 102 for Language. These sections share the same learning outcomes as other sections, and the courses themselves are as rigorous and challenging as other sections, but the students receive additional support given in the form of book clubs, regular meetings with a writing fellow (a peer trained by the Writing Studio in supporting peer writing, who works solely with students in a particular targeted section), and additional support sessions in the Academic Achievement Center. Students enrolled in these sections receive an additional credit (4 credits for the course instead of 3) to acknowledge the additional time spent in the book club and writing fellow meetings by co-enrolling in ENGL 144 (for ENGL 101) and ENGL 145 (for ENGL 102). Information about placement into these sections can be found later in this book.

First Year Seminar

First Year Seminars are writing intensive, topical courses that introduce students to academic thought and discourse. First Year Seminar (FYS) courses address learning outcomes designed to prepare and orient students toward productive and fulfilling college careers. These outcomes include the development of written fluency, the ability to read texts purposefully, and the capacity to gather topic-appropriate research materials.

All First Year Seminars are capped at 20 students so to enhance student to student and student to faculty discussions. In FYS, students are expected to develop their own arguments and defend them with supporting evidence through written and spoken communication. In this way, FYS courses introduce students to academic discourse, and students may choose or be asked to share their newly acquired knowledge with the college community at the Midyear Symposium.

As a central part of Bridgewater State University's Core Curriculum, all students must complete a three-credit First Year Seminar (FYS) within their first year (24 credits), ideally during their first semester on campus.

For more information go to http://www.bridgew.edu/fys/

Second Year Seminar

Second Year Seminars are a part of Bridgewater State University's Core Curriculum. Whereas First Year Seminar will introduce students to college-level thought and discourse, Second Year Seminar will engage students in a specific academic area of interest and provide students with the opportunity to reinforce, share and interpret knowledge. One way in which students might do that is through engagement with the outside world, such as a service learning project, a community-based research project, or field research.

Second Year Seminars (SYS) are 3 credit speaking-intensive (298) or writing-intensive (299), discipline-based topic courses that build on the academic skills and habits introduced in the first year of college at BSU. Students may take only one SYS course (either 298 or 299) for credit. The speaking-intensive SYS courses (298) have FYS, ENGL 101 and a speaking skills course (COMM 130 or THEA 210) as the prerequisites. The writing-intensive SYS courses (299) have FYS, ENGL 101 and ENGL 102 as the prerequisites.

For more information go to http://www.bridgew.edu/sys/

Placement Procedures for First-Year Writing Courses

The Academic Achievement Center uses various measures to ensure students that they are placed properly into mainstream or targeted sections of ENGL 101.

The following measures are used to determine placement in ENGL 101:

- A faculty-scored writing placement sample, written during New Student Orientation in response to a writing prompt.
- SAT-V scores: a score of 500-590 automatically places students in ENGL 101; a score of 600 or above automatically places a student in ENGL 102, exempting the student from ENGL 101; a score below 500 makes the student eligible for a targeted section of ENGL 101.
- ACCUPLACER Reading and Sentence Skills tests are administered to non-degree, transfer, international or continuing students needing placement, and any first-year student who missed the orientation writing sample opportunity. A combined Reading and Sentence Skills score below 153 automatically places a student in Targeted ENGL 101; a combined score above 153 places a student in a mainstream section of ENGL 101.

Students for whom English is an additional language and who are selected for a targeted section of ENGL 101 also have an opportunity to take ENGL 101 Targeted for Language. The benefits of taking this section include being taught by an instructor with specialized training in supporting second language students and being in a writing class with other second language students. Students who took this course in the past have reported feeling more comfortable speaking during class discussions and providing feedback to peer writing, as well as enjoying being in a class with peers who have had similar experiences writing across languages and cultures. International second language students with TOEFL scores under 550 are strongly encouraged to choose a Targeted for Language section of ENGL 101.

The English department also offers ENGL 102 Targeted for Language. Students enrolled in this section have the benefit of additional support through weekly book club and writing fellow meetings, as well as receive an additional course credit (receiving four rather than three credits, by co-enrolling in ENGL 145). The targeted for language section is especially beneficial for those English as a Second Language students who have not had as much experience writing researched essays and citing sources in Academic English.

Course Management Information

Attendance Policy

Each instructor will have an attendance policy stated on the syllabus. It is very important to be aware of this policy as excessive absences in most classes will result in a failure for the course or a lowered final grade.

Grading Policy

Each instructor will have a grading policy that outlines the criteria for determining a final grade for the course. In addition, the policy will inform students if late work is accepted and, if so, if there is a penalty for late work.

Midterm Progress Reports

At a determined time toward the middle of each semester, instructors are asked to submit warning grades for those students with a "D" or "F" grade. Instructors will notify students that these warning grades have been posted. In turn, students who receive such grades should set up an appointment with their instructors to discuss how more satisfactory progress can be achieved in the class.

Withdrawals

In some cases, the instructor or student may deem it advisable for the student to withdraw from the course once a warning grade has been given. The deadlines for withdrawal from a course occur in the weeks following midterm progress reports. Specific dates are available online at www.bridgew.edu/Registrar/withdrawal.cfm. They are also available along with withdrawal forms from the Registrar's Office on the ground level of Boyden Hall.

Incompletes

If a student wishes to apply to his or her instructor for a grade of IN (incomplete), this must be done in writing. Normally, incompletes are only given if circumstances beyond the control of the student occur after the official date for withdrawal from classes and if they impede completion of coursework by the end of the semester. Most of the coursework, however, should have already been completed. Both the instructor and student should agree on what remaining assignments must be completed, by when, and how these assignments will be collected and returned.

How to Handle Emergencies

It is an unfortunate occurrence whenever a student receives a failing grade for a course–especially if the failure could have been avoided. Should an unexpected emergency occur during the course of the semester, such as a serious physical illness for the student or a family member, a severe emotional problem, or a critical financial problem, the student should immediately set up an appointment with the instructor. Failing that, the student should immediately set up an appointment with the chair of the department the course is associated with. Students enrolled in ENGL 101 and ENGL 102 should set up an appointment with the chair of the English department, whose office hours will be posted on the door of Tillinghast 339. Students enrolled in FYS and SYS should use the college website to find the name and contact information of the chair for the department the course is associated with, and make an appointment. Depending on the circumstance, to avoid failing the course, a student may be advised to take a medical withdrawal, a regular withdrawal, or an incomplete. Meeting with the instructor or department chair will be much more effective than later trying to hand in multiple assignments or to request an incomplete at the end of the course after having been absent from class for several weeks. *Last minute requests without prior notification of the instructor about the emergency situation usually result in a failure for the course.*

Academic Integrity

Academic integrity refers to academic honesty–the avoidance of plagiarism or other forms of cheating. As stated in the *BSU Student Handbook*, "plagiarism and cheating are not condoned and are subject to academic penalty, which may result in a failure for the course in which the violation took place. A violation may result in a reduced grade, suspension, or dismissal from the college." (The entire policy can be found online at www.bridgew.edu/handbook/policiesprocedures/academicintegrity.htm.) The process is also detailed in the *Student Handbook*: the instructor, upon suspecting academic misconduct, has seven days to notify the student and meet to discuss the suspected infraction; the instructor then notifies the department chair and the associate vice president for academic affairs of both the infraction and the outcome of the meeting; in the case of repeat offenses, the student will go before the academic review panel. Students may also request that a case be brought before the academic review panel.

Instructors take cheating and plagiarism–the scholarly theft of words or ideas–very seriously. Most instructors will also see the handing in of the same paper to two teachers as cheating.

There are several things you can do to protect yourself from charges of academic misconduct. First, make sure you understand each instructor's definitions of cheating and plagiarism (which can shift slightly across the disciplines). If academic misconduct is not addressed on the instructor's syllabus or Moodle course page, be sure to ask. Second, before handing in an essay, you can run it through Safe Assign–a program available through Moodle that will check for close paraphrases and un-cited quotations, as well as language used in other student essays. You can then use the results to further revise the paper. Third, be sure to keep all drafts of your work. Save your paper often, using separate files to save brainstorming notes, early drafts, middle drafts, later drafts, and the final draft (i.e. Draft.1, Draft.2, Draft.3). Then, if an instructor asks you if a paper has been plagiarized, you can show the instructor the paper trail, which details how your ideas and language have evolved. The paper trail may also indicate accidental plagiarism–forgotten citations, un-cited paraphrases, paraphrases that use language too similar to the source. Many instructors will be more forgiving of accidental plagiarism than intentional plagiarism, asking you to revise to correct citations, rather than giving a failing grade to the paper.

Faculty Office Hours

All faculty members are expected to hold regular office hours and to state them on their office doors and in their syllabi. You should avail yourself of these hours for at least two reasons. First, visiting a professor during his or her office hours allows you to get to know each other better, which is helpful not only during the semester but also afterwards, when you may need to come back and ask for a letter of recommendation. (Most students need letters of recommendation at some point, whether it be for a job, a scholarship, or an application to graduate school.) Second, visiting professors during their office hours perhaps with an early draft of a paper or with some follow up questions from a class lets them know that you are a serious student and is beneficial to your learning.

Class Cancellations

Information on the cancellation of individual class meetings by an instructor will be provided on the hotline telephone number 508-531-1391 after 7:00 a.m. Absences may also be viewed on the Web at www.bridgew.edu by clicking on General Links under Current Students and then clicking on Faculty Absences. Cancellations due to inclement weather will be posted on the BSU homepage and announced at telephone number 508-531-1777, which will provide a message only in the event of class delay or cancellation.

Understanding a Course Syllabus

The course syllabi, which your college instructors pass out at the beginning of the semester, act as a contract between you and the instructor. Each syllabus provides information on the course goals, the instructor's expectations of the students for the semester, the kinds and dates of reading and writing assignments, and the formula by which the instructor will arrive at your final semester grade. Although individual syllabi may vary in the order in which this information is presented, they all provide this basic information for students.

Many instructors provide very detailed syllabi with additional information such as the nature of the learning styles applied in the course, the online materials students should have access to, and the date and time of the final examination. As you get your syllabi from instructors this semester, it is a good idea to go through them and underline or annotate information you know you will need.

It would also be a good idea for you to sit down with all your course syllabi at the beginning of the semester and create your own assignment calendar to keep track of the deadlines in all your courses. If you take time at the beginning of the semester to understand and collate the information from your course syllabi, you will save time later in the semester in planning your work. You will also avoid the embarrassment (and lowered grade) that results when you do not have an assignment completed on time.

Student Resources

Writing Studio

Location: Academic Achievement Center, bottom floor of Maxwell Library
Phone: 531-2053

The writing studio offers free consultations to provide students and faculty feedback on their writing (or to brainstorm ideas to write about later). Writers come to the studio for feedback on many types of work, including the following:

- works to be submitted for publication
- papers written for classes
- creative writing such as fiction and poetry
- personal statements written for graduate school applications
- resumes and cover letters

In addition to individual consultations on any of these types of writing, the writing studio offers the following free services:

- **Standing appointments** for writers who would like the structure of meeting with a consultant at the same time every week.
- **A library of handouts** with helpful hints on how to write effectively. To access these handouts, visit our Moodle website (VC 305-001 Writing Studio) or stop by the studio.
- **Links to several nationally-known online writing labs,** available on our Moodle website (VC 305-001 Writing Studio).
- **A library of handbooks** describing conventions for grammar, mechanics, punctuation, syntax, and citation styles (available for use in the Academic Achievement Center; ask a consultant for help finding a handbook that meets your needs).
- **A library of books discussing how to write in a variety of disciplines** (located behind our desk, to be used in the Academic Achievement Center for two-hour periods).
- **Classroom visitations** in which a consultant visits a class for five or ten minutes to give an overview of the services we offer or to give a brief lesson on a topic of interest to the students and professor.

- **Writers' Café,** an opportunity for BSU students to read their work aloud to an audience of appreciative faculty, students, and parents. Students may read fiction, creative non-fiction, poetry, or academic work (including short research papers or excerpts of longer papers). The Writers' Café is held once each semester. Submissions may be turned in at the Writing Studio desk in the Academic Achievement Center (bottom floor of Maxwell Library) or emailed to writingstudio@bridgew.edu; be sure to include your email address and phone number.

Making the Best Use of the Writing Studio

Here are some tips for making the best use of the Writing Studio:

- Bring your assignment sheet with you so that the consultant can see what criteria your professor will use to evaluate your work.

- Bring a print-out of your work; it's hard for consultants to give good feedback when reading on a computer screen. (If you don't have a print-out because you are at the brainstorming stage, that's fine.)

- Try not to wait until the day the paper is due to bring it to the studio. If you bring in your work several days *before* it's due, you'll have time to make substantive revisions rather than just a few random "quick fixes." In addition, any given consultation addresses only a limited number of issues, so consultants often recommend a follow-up appointment–something that you can't take advantage of when you bring in your work the day it is due.

- Bear in mind that the studio is a teaching unit, not a proofreading service. Writers who want feedback on grammar and punctuation can request that the consultant teach them how to find and correct these types of issues. Such work is a process rather than a quick fix and often requires a series of visits to the studio.

- Realize that the studio has a diverse staff of about 20 consultants. Feel free to work with different consultants until you find a good match for your specific needs as a writer.

Academic Achievement Center

Location: Bottom floor of Maxwell Library (by Starbucks) Phone: 531-1214

In addition to housing the Writing Studio, the Academic Achievement Center (AAC) houses the Communication Lab, Tutor Central for content tutoring in a variety of first-year courses, Disability Resources, Second Language Services, Mathematics Services, and Academic Coaching and Research Services. More information on each of these services is provided below.

Communication Lab (531-2225)

- Assists students with topic selection, outline, research, and with presentation practice

Content Tutoring Introductory Courses (531-1214)

- Supplementary assistance is provided by peer tutors through individual and group tutoring sessions.

Disability Resources (531-1713)

- Ensures all individuals equal access to BSU programs and services
- Offers a number of services to students who have a documented medical condition, are physically challenged, or have emotional or learning disabilities

If you anticipate that you will need disability support services, please contact Disability Resources at (508) 531-1713, TTY (508) 531-6113, or FAX (508) 531-5240. Disability Resources will work with you to evaluate your needs, determine resource availability, and assist in coordinating accommodations.

Second Language Services (531-2805)

Provides language support and tutoring for students for whom English is an additional language.

Students can sign up to meet with an English language tutor once per week throughout the semester. These tutoring sessions provide one-on-one language feedback specially tailored for each student. This is offered as a standalone service, or as a supplement to BSU's ENSL 101: Elementary English as a Second Language.

Students are also invited to take advantage of our walk-in appointments, where they receive support on specific academic assignments in the following areas:

- Fluency, accuracy, and creativity
- Cross cultural communication
- Spoken or written conversational and academic English

Mathematics Services (531-2013)

- Supports mastery of content in all mathematics courses

Academic Coaching and Research Services (531-2038)

- Teaches strategies for effective textbook study, note-taking, test-taking, and exam preparation
- Teaches effective research skills

Counseling Center

Location: Tillinghast 013 (In the hall between Health Services and the Mail Room)
Phone: 531-1331

Students may drop by or call the above number to make an appointment. Students visit the Counseling Center for many reasons, including the following:

- Feeling overwhelmed or stressed
- Concerns about relationships with friends, family, boyfriend/girlfriend
- A sense of sadness or hopelessness about a particular event
- Homesickness
- Feelings of anxiety, self-doubt, or depression
- Difficulty with motivation or procrastination
- Academic problems
- Difficulties with transitions
- Pregnancy concerns
- Difficulties with eating or sleeping
- Problems with alcohol or other drugs
- Eating disorders
- Rape, sexual assault, or relationship violence
- Suicidal thoughts
- Feeling that something is wrong and not being able to define it

The Counseling Center also offers couples counseling. In addition, online resources are available at www.bridgew.edu/CounselingCenter/. All counseling services at the Counseling Center are confidential.

Computer Support

BSU offers several options for assisting you with any issues you may have with your computer. Staff can repair and improve your laptop or iPad. Turnaround time is approximately 48 hours.

Technical Help Desks are available in Moakley 130 and on the ground floor of Maxwell Library. IT can be reached at x2555 (508-531-2555) or via email at: itsupport@bridgew.edu.

Your instructors will expect you to complete your work on time and regardless of any computer issues you face. Therefore, you can make use of any of the computer labs (in ground floor of Moakley and on the bottom floor of Harrington Hall) and areas (floors 1, 2, and 3 in Maxwell Library) while you wait for your computer to be returned to you.

Getting to Know the BSU Maxwell Library

Randi M. Rezendes

For many students, the library is a confusing and stress-inducing place. It may be associated with last-minute papers and frustrated research attempts. The purpose of this section is to challenge such ideas concerning the library and to help all BSU students see it as a source of help, inspiration, and information.

As a member of the BSU community, you have access to a vast collection of books and other materials; you may borrow materials (except when restrictions make it necessary to use items in the library only) to work with them outside of the library building. While you are required to find materials for class projects and papers, you are not limited to using the library for these purposes. Discovering what resources the library contains can help you build your knowledge base, develop new ideas, and follow research paths that will support and enhance your classroom learning and course projects.

Please read through the following information and then take some time to explore the information on your own before you have a project to do.

Getting Started

The Maxwell Library web page (www.bridgew.edu/Library/) has extensive information that will help you understand the resources available to you as a member of the BSU community.

Here are links to some basic information that will help you get started:

Library Hours and Events: www.bridgew.edu/Library/libevnt.cfm

Library Floor Plans: www.bridgew.edu/Library/1stfloor.cfm

Webster Online Catalog: http://webster.bridgew.edu/vwebv/searchBasic

Study Space

The Maxwell Library building, along with housing classrooms and university departments, contains a number of tables, chairs, and computers available for independent or collaborative work. It is a beneficial work space for individual or group study—a place where you can focus and avoid the distraction of home or the residence halls.

In addition to the open tables and chairs, the library has five Small Group Study Rooms throughout the building. These rooms are available to BSU students working in groups of two to six people. They cannot be reserved, but you can obtain access by visiting the Circulation Desk.

Please see the web page for more details on the Small Group Study Room policies and procedures: www.bridgew.edu/library/gstudyroom.cfm.

The Collections

While online searches via popular search engines can be helpful for brainstorming ideas, they do not always present scholarly, substantial, peer-reviewed sources that connect you to the work of experts in the field. When they do help you to find scholarly articles, these articles may not be available to you unless you subscribe to the specific journal that published the article. The items of the Maxwell Library collection have been selected by library staff or university faculty for their value in research and learning. Accessing these items through the library keeps you as a student from having to pay subscription fees that would be necessary to access these materials online. More information concerning the library's selection policy can be viewed online: www.bridgew.edu/Library/bkpolicy.cfm.

For the most part, the books of the library are organized using the *Library of Congress* system (see www.loc.gov/catdir/cpso/lcco/ for a list of classifications). The exception to this is the children's collection on second floor that follows the *Dewey Decimal* format favored by K-12 libraries that separates fiction and nonfiction (with fiction in alphabetical order and nonfiction with numerical designations).

In addition to books, the Maxwell Library also has a growing collection of media. Some of these can be seen in the *Media Room* (room 124), but the DVD collection is kept behind the circulation desk. To obtain a DVD, use the *Webster* catalog to find information, write down the name and call number, and bring them to the circulation desk with your connect card.

The library website includes further information on the various collections as well as information on accessing them:

> The Collections: www.bridgew.edu/Library/collections.cfm
>
> Webster Online Catalog: http://webster.bridgew.edu/vwebv/searchBasic
>
> Library Databases: http://maxguides.bridgew.edu/databases
>
> Journal and Newspaper List: http://atoz.ebsco.com/Titles/3490?lang=en&lang.menu=en&lang.subject=en

There are times that instructors will place an item or items on *Course Reserve* to limit the circulation of materials to enable a larger number of students to be able to access the material during the semester. Such materials are kept at the Circulation Desk. You may use the *Webster* catalog to find a list of course reserves by instructor. To access a course reserve, please bring the name of the item and the name of your instructor to the circulation desk along with your connect card. A member of the staff will get the item for you. Because course reserve materials are needed for a number of students, returning them in a timely manner is important to keep access open. For this reason, overdue course reserve materials will result in hourly (instead of daily) fines. Make sure that you return materials by the stated deadline in order to avoid such charges.

Access to Other Collections

There are times that the library collection will not have a specific title that you would like to access for a project. This does not mean that you have to give up hope of finding and using this item. The Maxwell Library online services enable you to request materials from college, university, and even public libraries:

ILL/DDS: www.bridgew.edu/Library/dds2.cfm
The Interlibrary Loan/Document Delivery Service allows you to gain access to articles that are not held by the Maxwell collection. Items are delivered electronically. You are notified via email with instructions on how to access the material.

MA Virtual Catalog: www.bridgew.edu/Library/massvirtual.cfm
The MA Virtual Catalog allows you to search other libraries in Massachusetts and request books, compact discs, films, and other materials from these libraries. Items are delivered to the BSU circulation desk. Once you are notified, you can pick them up using your connect card.

The Library Desks

The Maxwell Library has a wonderful staff that can help answer questions you have about navigating the library material and services. Please note three particular areas where staff members are available to assist you:

Circulation Desk: Located on the first floor of the library, just inside the main entrance to the Maxwell Library. It is where you will go with general library questions, to request a study room, to check out and return books, and to obtain course reserve materials and DVDs. You need your connect card to check out materials.

Circulation Desk: www.bridgew.edu/Library/circ.cfm
This link also includes information concerning library policies and procedures including borrowing limitations.

Reference Desk: Located on the first floor across from the circulation desk. The reference staff can help with research searches and help you locate materials in the library. For extensive research help, you can arrange an appointment with a reference librarian (see Reference Services link for details).

Reference Services: www.bridgew.edu/Library/ref.cfm

Educational Research Center—Located on the second floor near the Children's Collection. The ERC is a collection in the library that supports the professional education programs at BSU. It includes children's and young adult books as well as textbooks and other materials useful for educators and future educators. The staff of the ERC support this area of the library and can answer questions that you may have concerning it.

While the library staff is available for questions, there is extensive information available on the library pages, and there is a list of frequently asked questions. Please review these to see if you can find your answer. This will allow you to know where to find the information for yourself, and it will free the library staff to answer questions that are less common.

Frequently Asked Questions: www.bridgew.edu/Library/faq.cfm

In addition to the staff who are available during open library hours, the library has an online form that you can use to ask questions even when the library is closed.

Ask a Librarian: www.bridgew.edu/Library/askalib.cfm.

Library Scavenger Hunt

Ask your instructor if this will be used for a class assignment. If it isn't, you can use it to perform your own informal tour of the library.

Instructions: Print out a copy of the Library Floor Plan (or access it using a portable digital device): www.bridgew.edu/Library/1stfloor.cfm. Using this plan and the online catalog Webster catalog: http://webster.bridgew.edu/vwebv/searchBasic, answer the below questions below to help you explore.

Please keep these things in mind while completing this activity:

- You are welcome to check out any titles that are of interest to you. They do not have to be a part of an assigned class project.
- Please be respectful while in the library. Quiet discussion with a partner is acceptable, but you should keep your volume down and not talk on your cell phone while walking through the library.
- If you take any books off the shelves and do not take them out, please leave them on the wood carts that are scattered around the library. They will be put back on the shelves by the library staff who will make sure the books are put back in the appropriate places.

Partner Option: You may work on this activity with a partner, but each of you should complete your own worksheet. If this is a class assignment, each of you will be expected to pass it in. Each of you should choose your own books on questions that include such options. This makes the scavenger hunt something that is useful to you as an individual.

1. In the library, books that are taken off the shelves but not checked out should not be put back on the shelves by patrons. Instead, they should be placed on the wood carts that are designated for this purpose. There are carts like these on each floor of the library. Where are they?

2. Find the display of new book additions on the first floor. Name at least two books that are of interest to you (include title, author, and call number). Why do they interest you?

3. Find the display of books for leisure reading that is also located on the first floor. Name at least one book that interests you (include title, author, and call number). Why does it grab your attention?

4. Find the media room (room 124) on the first floor. Is there anything of interest for you there? If so, what is it? Please include the title, author, call number, and format. Why is it of interest to you?

5. Use your laptop or a library computer to access the Webster online catalog (see link above). Find one DVD the library has that could be of interest to you. Please include the title and call number. [Note: You can try searching for a favorite actor or director to see what the library has in connection with this person.] Please note the title and call number below. Why have you chosen this title?

6. Where are the group study rooms? How many are there and what is the procedure for using one?

7. Print out the library floor plan handouts (or download them to a portable digital device). Use these plans to identify the different subject areas for the library's general collection. Which section could be of interest to you because of your major or hobbies? Find that area and list at least two books that interest you (include title, author, and call number). Why do they grab your attention?

8. Which floor of the library does not contain any bathrooms? Where are the bathrooms located on the other floors?

9. Find the children's collection on the second floor. Select at least one book that interests you (include title, author, and call number). Why does it grab your attention?

10. Walk around the library and write about three things that you discover that could be of personal or academic use to you. Explain the reasons for your choices.

Places to Publish and Present

Sharing your work with a wider audience can be immensely gratifying. Not only is it a real pleasure to discover that readers outside of the classroom find value in your work, but the experience can add to your confidence as a writer, empowering you to continue writing and seeking wider audiences. Bridgewater State University offers a wealth of venues for sharing your writing with a wider audience, both in print and through public readings. Below, we have listed a number of venues that accept work from first-year students, but as you continue through your college career, you will discover even more venues, such as newsletters, journals, and conferences dedicated to specific majors.

Student Publication Venues

The Bridge

The Bridge, BSU's student run-literature and fine arts journal, is an annual volume of student fiction, creative non-fiction, poetry and visual art. Each year since its inception, *The Bridge* has won prestigious awards from the Columbia Scholastic Press Association. Submissions are accepted between the end of April and the last day of the fall semester. For details about submissions and to view past volumes of *The Bridge,* go to www.thebridgejournal.com. Send inquiries to thebridgejournal@bridgew.edu.

The Comment

The Comment, BSU's student-run newspaper, encourages students unaffiliated with the newspaper to submit editorials and articles. Letters to the editors and articles can be sent by email to comment@bridgew.edu. You can also drop off a hard copy of an article at *The Comment* office in Campus Center 103. If you are interested in applying for a staff position, inquire at *The Comment* office or send an email.

Embracing Writing

Embracing Writing, the volume you are currently reading, publishes student work written in English 101, English 102, the First Year Seminar, and the Second Year Seminar. Awards are given for excellence in the following categories in 101 or 102: Expository or Persuasive Writing, Creative Non-Fiction, and Researched Writing. Awards are also given in the following categories: Excellence in First Year Seminar Writing, Excellence in Second Year Seminar

Writing, Excellence in Writing Quantitative Argument, and Excellence in Writing on the Topic of Sustainability. The first place winner in each category receives $50 and guaranteed publication in the next edition of *Embracing Writing*. For more information about the submission process, please see the last page in this book. If you have any questions, contact Dr. Julia Stakhnevich at (508) 531-2805 or at jstakhnevich@bridgew.edu.

The Undergraduate Review

The Undergraduate Review, administered by the Adrian Tinsley Program for Undergraduate Research, publishes student research and creative work done as part of a class or under the mentorship of BSU faculty. Published annually, this journal features work from students across the college and has space set aside for work from first-year students. For details about the submission process and deadlines, go to www.bridgew.edu/ATP/ur.cfm.

Student Presentation Venues

Midyear Symposium of First and Second Year Student Work

Sponsored by the Office of Undergraduate Research, the Midyear Symposium features work by first and second year students. This event, held at the end of fall semester, is open to both creative and research projects, and both oral and poster presentations. Beginning in October, there will be a link on our page to submit your abstract electronically. To see what past years' participants have done, go to www.bridgew.edu/OUR/MYS/midyearsymposium. cfm. For further information about the event, contact the Office of Undergraduate Research at 508.531.2303. If you are interested in presenting at the symposium, you should talk to the instructor of the course for which you did the work you want to present. More information will be available on the OUR website.

Undergraduate Research Symposium

Sponsored by the Adrian Tinsley Program and the Office of Undergraduate Research, the Undergraduate Research Symposium features both research and creative work by students from across the college. The Symposium is held near the end of spring semester; look for dates and deadlines for this event in spring. All BSU undergraduate students, regardless of major or year, are encouraged to participate, and faculty are welcome to invite their classes to attend all or part of the Symposium. For more information about the proposal process and the event, go to www.bridgew.edu/ATP/symposiumgeninfo.cfm.

The Writer's Café

Sponsored by the Writing Studio and the Academic Achievement Center, The Writer's Café provides a forum for you to read your work aloud to an appreciative audience. You may submit fiction, creative non-fiction, poetry, or academic work, including short research papers or excepts of longer papers. You may submit multiple pieces, and you may submit work every semester. Note that many writers who read at The Writer's Café go on to become consultants in the Writing Studio. The Writer's Café is held once each semester. In the fall, The Writer's Café will be held in November. Please check the Writing Studio web page for dates and submission deadlines. For spring, the submission deadline and Writer's Café dates may be found on the Writing Studio's webpage. For both the spring and the fall submissions may be emailed directly to writingstudio@bridgew.edu. Please be sure to include your full name along with your submission. Details can be found by clicking The Writer's Café link on the Writing Studio's website: http://www.bridgew.edu/WritingStudio/.

National Conference on Undergraduate Research (NCUR)

Since its inception in 1987, NCUR has become a major annual event drawing over 2,500 undergraduates, faculty, and administrators from over 300 colleges and universities across the country to present, hear, and discuss undergraduate creative and scholarly work. Each year, a number of BSU undergraduate proposals are accepted. To simplify travel and reduce costs, the group travels together to NCUR. For more information, go to www.bridgew.edu/ATP/ncur.cfm. While it is not often that first year work is accepted for presentation at this conference, this event is still good to keep in mind as you continue with your academic career.

National Day on Writing

To celebrate writing in all of its forms, BSU participates in the National Day on Writing (NDoW), which usually takes place on October 20th or shortly after. This annual celebration was initiated by the National Council for Teachers of English (NCTE) and at BSU consists of a full day of public readings, sponsored by different groups. As part of the celebration, students are invited to share with others their own writing by reading it out loud or by participating in reading presentations of the works by other authors whom they admire. NDoW celebrates writing of all genres—from shopping lists to blogs to memos to poems to short stories and everything in between. Interested students should contact their writing instructor or the English department for more information.

Helpful Strategies for Writing

College Writing—Navigating the Transition

Shelagh M. Smith

Whether you are emerging from high school or returning to college after raising a family or being in the workforce, college writing is going to challenge you in ways you probably had not previously considered. College writing—*or writing for an academic audience*—is quite different than some of the writing you have completed in other circumstances.

Gone are the days of the five-paragraph essay. Similarly, gone are the days of quickly jotted emails and texts to friends, where conventions of written discourse (primarily grammar and spelling) are not a priority. In academic writing, everything you write—every word you use, every punctuation mark you choose—is going to be evaluated. Here are some guidelines to help you navigate that transition.

The basic differences between non-academic writing and academic writing can be summed up in the **Four E's – Express, Expand, Engage, and Evaluate.**

Express Your Ideas

In nearly every class, you will be expected to contribute to the discussion by expressing your opinions on a wide variety of subjects. And in most classes, you will be asked to express your ideas in writing, whether in an essay format, a business report, a lab report, or another type of college-level writing assignment.

During this first stage of expressing ourselves, every idea sounds "great," but in reality, most of our initial ideas are knee-jerk reactions to a specific situation, question, or writing prompt. They bear little resemblance to the final product you will be expected to turn in. In college, great ideas are not enough. The seed of your idea can get you started, but in academic writing you are expected to go beyond that and nurture your seed into a beautiful garden. That nurturing comes through a series of steps outlined below.

Expand Your Ideas

Part of academic writing is the willingness to participate in critical thinking, which means you are expected to go beyond the surface of what you have read (and what you might write) on any given subject. *You must question everything—especially yourself.* Ask yourself why you feel the way you do about a particular subject. Is it an idea that stems from deep emotion or past experiences? Now go beyond that. Discover what others feel about the subject. So, for example, if you are writing an opinion paper on the death penalty and you are a supporter, ask yourself why you feel the way you do. Who else do you know who feels the same way? Are your ideas are deeply embedded in family history? In other words, do you feel that way because that's the way your family feels? Ask yourself if you know enough about your idea to fully support it.

Now take it one step further. Learn as much as you can about your subject. Read newspapers or textbooks or scholarly articles on it; visit online forums to see what others are saying on the subject. This should help solidify your concept, but be warned that it will likely not be enough to create a solid piece of writing. You must dig even deeper.

Engage with Others

Part of being an academic writer (and thinker) is embracing a willingness to engage with others who might not share the same views. It is important that you not only present your ideas, but that you present them in a way that acknowledges another viewpoint. You don't have to agree with an alternate view, but you do have to consider it. The first step toward that consideration is applying critical thinking to your sources and engaging with others in what is essentially a "conversation."

Writers write to be read. In other words, they write to get feedback, either positive or negative, from readers. Readers are supposed to question what they read; hopefully, they feel strongly enough about the subject that they either agree wholeheartedly, or disagree vehemently. When that agreement or disagreement occurs, that is called "joining the conversation," or engaging with the text. Most of your engagement will come in the written form, where you will be asked to consider a subject, find resources, and create a written response to the question at hand, but there will be other times when that engagement will come in class, during class discussions. That is why it is important to learn as much as you can about your subject so you can present a well-informed opinion with evidence that will withstand scrutiny. Remember, it is not enough to simply write (or say), "This is what I believe, so you must believe it, too." You must prove it.

So when your professor hands you a reading or a textbook, or (continuing with the earlier example) if you find an article opposing the death penalty, ask critical questions: Who wrote it? Why did he or she write it? What is it about? How is it supported? When was it written? Who is paying for or commissioning the article? What does it mean? *Engage with the material as though it is a person speaking directly to you, but only this conversation takes place on paper.*

And when it comes time to write your response, put all of that critical thinking on paper. Prove your point. Expand and engage on your subject so that anyone who reads your work will have a full understanding of not only what you're trying to say, but *why* you're saying it. Then, prepare to pose those same questions to your own work as you engage in the final step.

Evaluating Your Work

This step is, without a doubt, one of the most important—and often most difficult—steps in the academic writing process. In this step, you must turn your critical thinking skills toward your own ideas and the way they are presented. Many novice academic writers tend to put their ideas down on paper, breathe a sigh of relief, and wash their hands of the process, turning it over to the professor for their evaluation. But your own evaluation of your work is just as critical to your success.

Once you've finished your first draft, take your idea, take your research, and ask yourself if it makes sense, not just to you, but to anyone unfamiliar with your subject. Ask yourself some tough questions:

- Is my position debatable? Are there two reasonable sides to this argument?

- Is my position presented logically and laid out in a way that will make the most sense to my reader?

- Are my sources reliable? Do they meet the required standards for academic sources? Have I utilized the best tools to help me present my case? Have I visited the Maxwell Library and used its resources to their fullest extent? (See "Getting to Know the BSU Maxwell Library")

- Does my work go beyond feelings and emotion? Can I prove everything I say? Do I have enough evidence to convince a reader that my ideas have merit? And beyond evidence, do I make it clear *why* my ideas are important? What are my reasons for feeling this way, and are they relatable to my audience?

- Are my sources doing the work I hoped they would? Do they back me up or undermine my position?

- And is my writing truly "college level" in terms of meeting academic discourse requirements? Is it proofread? Is it meeting the criteria laid out by the instructor? Does it adhere to standard academic conventions of formatting? Am I delivering it in a way that is acceptable to the audience (instructor and/or class)?

- Do I need to visit the Academic Achievement Center for support with my writing?

If you can answer adequately to most of these questions, you're ready to take that final step and turn in your work. But do remember that first drafts are rarely acceptable. There are no first drafts on the New York Times Bestseller List, and there are even fewer first drafts in the "A" column of a professor's gradebook.

Now, of course, there will be other differences between the writing you've done in the past and what you're expected to do in college, and many of those differences will fall into the category of basic mechanics. Your professors will expect your work to be typed and printed out for class (or posted in an online forum); they will expect it to be proofread carefully (that means *read with your eyes*, not with spell check); and they will expect it to be free of slang and text speak (ya im tlkng 2U). Your professors will also expect your sources to be credible and cited appropriately in a specific citation style.

But perhaps the biggest difference between college writing and high school writing is the final, unspoken E. ***Effort.*** College is a time for you to expand your ideas, your horizons, and your experiences, and part of that expansion is how you approach your writing (and thinking). Unlike high school, there are very few professors who will hand you the answers or spend entire weeks working on papers in class. Your instructors will give you the guidelines, they will show you how it's done, but they will not do it for you. That responsibility falls squarely on your shoulders. Most of your longer writing assignments should be completed on your own time outside of class. It is up to you to budget your time and resources accordingly and to apply those critical thinking skills to how you manage your workload.

How well you do in college writing (and college in general) depends heavily on how much effort you are willing to put into your work. If you give your ideas—and your academic work—the time and respect they deserve, it's likely your professors will, too.

Writing Rhetorically

Michelle Cox and Anne Doyle

What does it mean to write rhetorically? It means to write with an awareness of your readers, of your intentions as a writer, and of how your writing may be interpreted.

Some may interpret "rhetoric" only to apply to persuasive writing. Indeed, rhetoric is most visibly at work when the writer is trying to persuade the reader to agree with a specific stance or move the reader to take a specific action.

And yet *all* writing that is meant to be read by another is rhetorical. Consider the ways in which a writer when writing a memoir uses language to create a persona and to convince the readers that the slices of life presented in the work are true, really happened, in just the way they have been told in the memoir. All of these moves rely on rhetoric. Consider the ways in which a fiction writer persuades the reader to suspend his/her disbelief and be taken in by the world unfolding in the pages, so taken in that the characters' lives and emotions touch the reader. These moves too are rhetorical. Whenever we write, we unconsciously consider rhetoric, but when we use knowledge of rhetoric to guide the choices we make as writers, our writing becomes more effective, more powerful, more likely to move our readers in the ways we intend.

An awareness of rhetoric also helps us write into unfamiliar rhetorical situations. College writing is full of unfamiliar situations. Emphasizing this point, Lucille Parkinson McCarthy entitled her article detailing a college student's experiences writing in courses across the curriculum "A Stranger in Strange Lands." An awareness of rhetoric can help new terrain feel less "strange," as it provides approaches for navigating new rhetorical spaces. Rhetoric can even provide heuristics–guiding questions–for figuring out approaches to unfamiliar writing situations. Who is the target audience? What does the reader already know about this topic? What does the reader care about? What voice would be most effective for establishing my credibility (ethos) with this reader? What genre is the reader expecting? What does this genre typically look like? How can I most effectively use the conventions of this genre to communicate effectively to the reader? For what purpose would the reader be reading my text? What do I most want the reader to know, think about, or do? How can I emphasize this focus through the organization of my text?

Here are a few concepts useful for developing rhetorical awareness:

Rhetorical situation: The rhetorical situation is the coming together of the writer, the audience, the topic, and the writer's purpose for addressing that audience. Rhetorician Lloyd Bitzer speaks of the situation as arising out of **exigency**, that is, out of the writer's need to address that audience on that topic for that purpose. According to Bitzer, it is this exigency which drives the act of writing. For example, when my elderly aunt sends me a Christmas present, I know I need to send her a thank you note. My exigency is my awareness that my aunt (audience) expects me (the writer) to say thanks (my purpose) for the present (my topic); if I don't write that note, her feelings will be hurt.

Primary audience/target audience: This is the group of readers you are most focused on when writing, the group that you most want to hear your message, read and take in your words. They are the group who will be affected by your words, which may stir them to action, provide them with information, entertain or enlighten them, etc.

Secondary audience: This is the additional group of readers who may also read your piece of writing (for example, a recommendation report you wrote for your employer may also be read by the employer's assistants). Though not your intended audience, the secondary audience is still an important group of readers to consider. In fact, sometimes a writer will mask the primary audience as the secondary audience. You may have noticed this rhetorical move in advertisements for food products marketed to children. The commercial shows happy children eating the food and asking the parent for more food, while the overlaid voice, though using a sappy tone meant to grab children's attention, spells out the food's health benefits and reasonable cost. Though ostensibly aimed at children, the commercial's real audience is the parents, who have the means to go to the grocery store and purchase the food.

Message: What we see in this example of the child-centered food commercial is an instance of adapting the message to the ostensible secondary audience. The message is the heart of a text: it is what we are trying to convey to the readers. When we consider the parents as the real audience of the food commercial, we can see how the message (this food is nutritious and inexpensive) is adapted-through a high, sappy voice–to appeal to the ostensible primary audience, the children. Notice how the message is linked to the purpose of the discourse: the purpose of the commercial is to convince listeners to buy the food product, while the message about nutrition and cost is intended to be the persuasive mechanism of the discourse.

Genre: At its simplest, we can think of genre as "kind of writing": fiction, poetry, report, memoir, essay, letter, text message, web page, blog entry, caption, manual, etc. Of course, when we look more closely at any of these "kinds of writing," we realize they can be further narrowed down into short story, novel, flash fiction (fiction); sonnet, epic, haiku, etc. (poetry); thank you, sales letter, bad news letter, good news letter (letter), sales report, recommendation report, lab report, book report, etc. (report), and so on. Although these genres often appear to be empty forms into which the writer pours words, genres are more dynamic and more interesting than that. Many researchers today speak of genre as a type of social action (Miller; Devitt). By doing so, they recognize that the genre in which you choose to convey your message to your audience is itself a part of the persuasion; in that sense, it is a social action because it has a real affect on the audience. Choice of genre can let your audience know if you are an "insider" or an "outsider"–that is, whether you know what sort of genre is usually used for such a message to this particular audience. Think about your own experiences: You would probably write a letter to the dean requesting a waiver of a particular school requirement, but you might simply write an email note to a professor indicating that you needed another copy of the class assignment. But if you are a salesperson letting your boss know how much you've sold in the past month, you would write a sales report. A writer's ability to choose the right genre for the audience and the situation is crucial.

Context: The context of any argument is a combination of circumstances: the audience, the writer's intentions or purpose, and the surrounding situation–that is, the location and the time of the argument. Context may also include what has been said already on the subject. For example, for anyone in the United States writing on the subject of abortion, the lengthy dispute between the concepts of Right to Life and Right to Choose forms part of the context for writing. Context can also include differences in power between audience and writer. For example, a teenager writing an email to convince parents to allow the teenager to spend the night at a friend's is in a very different power position from an employer writing a set of guidelines for the office staff regarding filing practices in the office. The teen knows the audience for the email has the power to say "No," while the employer knows that the employees in the office will have a hard time refusing to implement the guidelines being suggested.

Appeal to ethos: This and the following two appeals were identified by Aristotle in his influential work on rhetoric and speech, which we also apply to writing. Ethos refers to a writer's character or persona as represented in a piece of writing. With this move, the writer is implying, *trust me, because I'm the one making the argument.* An appeal to ethos is most evident when a writer names his/her credentials in a piece. For instance, in the student essay on euthanasia in animal shelters included in this book, "To Kill or Not to Kill," Meagan Gardiner tells us of her own experience volunteering in such shelters, a move that persuades the reader of the credibility of this writer. Ethos may also be established through the use of secondary sources (a move that tells the reader to trust the writer as the writer has done a great deal of research), but only if the sources themselves are credible. An uncritical citation of *Wikipedia, About.com,* or *Dictionary.com* may hurt a writer's ethos. Ethos may also be established through voice, which is discussed in detail below.

Appeal to logos: This appeal refers to moves a writer makes to persuade readers based on fact or soundness of reason. With this move, the writer is implying, *trust me, because the facts speak for themselves.* An appeal to logos is most evident when the writer cites statistics or other types of numerical information. Of course, facts never speak for themselves, so the writer must make connections for readers between the facts and the claims. If you took Foundations in Logic and Reasoning, this is the appeal that you learned about in the course. As explained in this course, logos refers not only to facts, but to the ways that arguments are organized, methods of organization that have been endlessly classified and analyzed. More important than the names of different types of arguments is the readers' response to your argument–whether readers find the argument well-reasoned and credible. Readers tend to find arguments well-reasoned when the thesis (main point being argued) is clear and makes sense, and each claim (statement supporting the argument) is backed by credible evidence.

Appeal to pathos: This appeal refers to moves a writer makes to pull on the readers' emotions in relation to the argument. With this move, the writer is implying, *trust me, because the argument affects you in some way.* In 2008, when the question to close greyhound race tracks was on the Massachusetts ballot, proponents of the question handed out flyers that listed the animal advocacy groups endorsing the flyer (ethos), and statistics displaying the number of dogs endangered by racing (logos), but I'm willing to bet that it was the photograph of a sad-eyed greyhound featured prominently at the top of the flyer that won over voters' hearts, ultimately persuading them to support the bill, thus ending greyhound racing in Massachusetts. As much as we are persuaded by a writer's credibility and the soundness of an argument, feelings are eminently persuasive, so much so that many commercials (arguments to persuade consumers to spend money on their products) make heavy use of appeals to pathos: buy this product and feel younger, buy this product and be more attractive to others.

Kairos: Timing is particularly significant in argument. The ancient Greek rhetoricians spoke about two different kinds of time: **chronos**, which is just the passage of time, and **kairos**, which is the acknowledgement that there are more and less appropriate times for some arguments. A writer who understands the significance of kairos knows that sometimes a specific audience is more or less prepared to consider a specific argument. For example, in the 1990s, few Americans were ready to listen to arguments about a need for stricter investment controls on brokerages, mortgage companies, or banks. But by 2009, after the implosion of the stock market, the collapse of the housing bubble, and the need to bail out several major banks, many Americans became willing to consider arguments for investment reform.

Of course, knowing that the time is not ripe for a particular argument should not stop you from making the argument, but you would probably seek to get your audience to see that there are flaws in the current situation. For example, given the recent election of Barack Obama as the first Black U.S. president, many Americans currently claim that there is no longer a real problem with racism in this country. Someone wishing to argue for the maintenance or extension of affirmative action programs in this climate would need to prove that there still is a significant problem, perhaps by demonstrating how few Black Americans, proportionately, receive the education and have the career opportunities of a Michelle or Barack Obama.

Register: Register is a social concept, having to do with degree of formality in language choice. For example, you could choose a very breezy, informal kind of language or a more formal, or "frozen," style. (Linguist Martin Joos calls language "frozen" when it is highly formal and attempts to freeze meaning into place. For example, laws are usually written in "frozen" language, as was the U.S. Constitution and the Declaration of Independence. You might say that the most formal language is used when the writer(s) believe they are formally writing for posterity.) For most undergraduate college writing, your readers will expect you to use a middle register: not too casual, but not stuffy, either. Consider the following:

> Informal: My buds and I heard our prof was out sick and the test was deep-sixed. We chilled.

> Middle: When my classmates and I heard our teacher was ill and the test was cancelled, we relaxed.

> Formal: When the members of my class became aware that our teacher was ill and the test would not be administered to us, we were greatly relieved.

You may be asked to keep readers' journals, response journals, or do other first-person reflective writing. The instructor assigning this writing should let you know how informal (or formal) the reflections should be.

Voice: A complex concept, voice involves both tone and style. Readers respond strongly to voice, deciding whether a writer is someone to trust, someone entertaining, someone worth listening to. A writer's voice is conveyed to the readers by means of *all* the stylistic, register and word choices the author has made. Generally, a writer wants to be perceived by the readers as a person of good sense, sound information, and of good will toward the reader (in other words, a person of good **ethos**.) Voice goes beyond these basics: for example, through careful pronoun selection, the writer can establish a common identity with the reader (using *we*) or establish the writer as an expert giving advice to less experienced readers (using *you*). The writer's word choice can establish the writer as a discerning individual (for example, by describing a building as "leaning its cracked concrete walls against its neighbors in sheer exhaustion" instead of "being old and run-down.") The writer's voice can be pompous, friendly, angry, humorous, etc.

Using Rhetorical Awareness during the Writing Process

Some writers find that thinking about rhetoric too early in the writing process may cause them to experience writer's block. The reader hovers too long over that blank page, threatening to critique each turn of phrase, each idea, each word. Compositionist Peter Elbow tells us to "close our eyes and write" when this happens–force ourselves to freewrite, writing so quickly, without concern for sentence structure, style, soundness of idea, that we learn to ignore that internalized critic. And compositionist and journalist Donald Murray would tell us to "lower your expectations"–sage advice that helps many writers move past our feelings of incompetence in the face of what we think our readers expect of us. On the other hand, an awareness of readers does not always stop us from writing, but can rather ignite our writing, providing that muse that pushes us to write. In fact, I would not be writing these words now–and thereby sorting out my own ideas of what it means to write rhetorically and why rhetorical awareness matters–if I did not feel compelled to do so by your imagined presence.

Rhetorical awareness is particularly useful during the revision process. How can we know how to revise to improve the effectiveness of our writing without reader feedback? Some instructors will build opportunities for reader feedback into a course, by providing their own feedback to your writing to early drafts and holding workshops during class to provide peer review. If not, seek out feedback at the Writing Studio, a place on campus where all students may receive feedback from trained peer readers on writing in any stage of the writing process. You may also find it helpful to receive feedback from family and friends, but be aware that those who are close to us may only provide "comfort readings"–positive but uncritical feedback that doesn't push our writing along.

Knowledge of rhetoric can determine your success in writing assignments. A low grade on a writing assignment often indicates that the writer misread the assignment's rhetorical situation–selected a genre, register, style of argument that the instructor was not anticipating. If a writing assignment description does not include information about the rhetorical situation, be sure to ask the instructor about what she/he is envisioning in terms of genre conventions, target audience, evidence, and register. Asking the instructor for examples of successful student papers written from the same assignment or published work exemplifying the moves the instructor is expecting would also be helpful to you in reading the rhetorical situation of the assignment.

Writing is a complex interchange between writer and readers, an interchange that takes place within a specific rhetorical situation, time, and place. It is rhetoric that moves writing from being formulaic to being responsive to the dynamic situation it is a part of. And it is rhetorical awareness that moves a writer from being merely competent to being adept in the face of the many challenging demands of writing across courses, audiences, genres, situations, registers, and disciplines. To write well is, in the end, to write with rhetorical savvy.

Works Cited

Aristotle. *The Art of Rhetoric*. Trans. Hugh Lawson-Tancred. New York: Penguin Classics, 1992.

Bitzer, Lloyd. "The Rhetorical Situation." *Philosophy and Rhetoric 1* (January 1968): 1–14.

Devitt, Amy J. *Writing Genres*. Carbondale, IL: Southern Illinois UP, 2004.

Elbow, Peter. "Closing My Eyes as I Speak: An Argument for Ignoring Audience." *College English 49* (1): 50–69.

Joos, Martin. *The Five Clocks*. New York: Harcourt, Brace, & World, 1967.

McCarthy, Lucille Parkinson. "A Stranger in Strange Lands: A College Student Writing across the Curriculum." *Research in the Teaching of English 21*(3) (1987): 233–65.

Miller, Carolyn R. "Genre as Social Action." 1984. *Genre and the New Rhetoric*. Ed. Aviva Freedman and Peter Medway. Bristol, PA: Taylor and Francis, 1994. 23–42.

Murray, Donald. *Expecting the Unexpected: Teaching Myself–and Others–to Read and Write*. Boston: Boynton/Cook, 1989.

Writing Rhetorically in Digital Spaces

Jennifer A. Fallas and Randi M. Rezendes

When you think of writing rhetorically, you may often think of research papers or persuasive essays, but the technological advances of our society have provided us with new spaces in which to write. These digital spaces allow us to connect with others and exchange ideas in a variety of ways.

Since electronic writing such as text messaging, emails, profile updating, and social networking is probably a part of your personal life, it is easy to forget that these forms of communication, when used in connection with classes, assignments, and scholarly discourse, are your academic (and eventually professional) representation. For this reason, it is important to have an awareness of the rhetorical context of writing situations or assignments that take place in these digital spaces. In this section, we will discuss three digital genres: email, blogs, and discussion forums, to explore the rhetorical needs and potential pitfalls of each situation.

A note about presentation and word choice:

Although you may use these formats for informal writing for your own personal purposes, these genres, when used in connection with an academic course or assignment, are spaces of academic writing that reflect you as a writer and scholar. To represent yourself in the clearest and most professional way possible, you should follow the conventions of Standard Written English when writing using any of these methods. Usage of slang (sup?), textspeak abbreviations (LOL, IDK, btw), emoticons (☺) and lack of capital letters in appropriate places (including the personal pronoun *I*) or lack of punctuation detract from the presentation of your writing and may cause your ideas to be misinterpreted by your instructor or peers.

Email Communication

It is important to understand how to construct effective and appropriate emails to your instructors (and other university officials and administrators). Email communication with university professionals or personnel, while a convenient and quick method, is still a written form of communication that represents you as a student. Following format and content guidelines allows the receiver to see the care you have taken in writing the message and may allow your message to be understood without the need to try and decipher words and meaning.

Your instructors will provide you with a course syllabus on the first day/week of class. If an instructor has specific communication instructions or a preferred method of communication, it will be on the syllabus. Paying attention to these sections and using preferred channels and formats will often allow you to avoid missed communications and misunderstandings between you and your recipients. Prior to sending any email, always double-check your course syllabus (or online course e-learning site if applicable) for the answer or feedback you're seeking. It is likely that you will be able to find answers for most of your questions or concerns regarding your courses in those sections.

When sending emails to university professionals or personnel, it is useful to include the following information:

- Use your BSU email account whenever possible and check it regularly. By using this account, school personnel will more readily recognize your email address and understand it has something to do with BSU. This is particularly important because, if you are using a personal email account rather than your BSU account, there is the risk that university personnel might mistake your legitimate email as a spam message to be discarded. Checking your BSU email account on a regular basis will help you make sure that you do not miss important correspondence and responses to the message you send.

- In the "Subject" line: Include your first and last names and course information (i.e. ENGL 254-110). Instructors usually teach more than one class per semester and often teach several sections of the same course. By including the full number designation and department information, the instructor will be able to better help you.

- Begin your email with an appropriate greeting and address your instructor by his or her title (i.e., "Professor" or "Doctor"). Titles that indicate one's relationship status (i.e., "Mrs.," "Mr.," or "Ms") are inappropriate.

- If your email is something quick, it is best to keep your emails concise and to the point. Provide enough background why you're writing and what it is you need help with, along with a question specific to your concerns.

  - For example: "I am in your Writing about Film class that meets on Mon, Wed, Fri from 12-1250. I have looked through our syllabus and am unable to find the title of the reading due for next class. Could you please remind me what it is?"

- Generally, if you have a longer query for your instructor, it is best to speak to him or her in person. While email communication seems like a quick way to discuss the matter, back-and-forth discussions via email actually takes more time than face-to-face discussions because the correspondents may not be online at the same time and often have other messages to address. A face-to-face meeting allows a designated time to discuss the matter. You can let your instructor know you have a concern that will require some time and ask for a meeting time (preferably during his or her office hours).

  - For example: "I have some concerns about my progress in your course. I'd like to make an appointment to speak with you during your office hours or at another mutually agreeable day and time."

- Much as your instructor's preferred method of communication will be listed on your syllabus, he or she will also detail whether assignments may be submitted via email. Always check course guidelines or ask your instructor for this policy prior to emailing any assignments. When sending assignments or other materials, do so as attachments (unless otherwise directed by your instructor) and make sure that the attachment is the appropriate file type your instructor wants.

- Finish your email with a closing as you would any letter. Even though BSU accounts are designated by your first initial and last name, there are often several other persons on campus with the same or similar initials and last names and this might be confusing for the recipient of your email and would likely delay a response to your query.

  - For example: Cordially, Your name here

Writing Rhetorically in Digital Spaces

Further Information

- For further information regarding BSU's policy regarding email as *communication*, see: http://it.bridgew.edu/Policy/EmailCommPolicy.cfm

- For further information regarding BSU's policy regarding email *use* in general, see: http://it.bridgew.edu/Policy/Email.cfm

Blogs

Many instructors (although not all) utilize blogs (and/or other social networking sites) as assignments or part of assignments. As a student, you may be expected to write blog posts of your own or comment on a blog that's already published by using the "comment" function.

Instructors use blogs as writing spaces. Blogs help to connect the genre of rhetorical writing you do in your writing courses with the format of social networking sites with which you are no doubt already familiar. In blog assignments, you will work independently and collaboratively to craft and respond to written pieces. Blogs allow writers and readers to interact with and modify the writing(s) while working together to generate and think analytically about the content.

Blogging, blog commenting, and other social networking entries follow most of the same rules that apply to any other writing assignment you'll write in your courses. Your tone, formatting, organization, spelling, grammar, and punctuation are all key to getting your message across. Most of the time, your instructors and peers will be your reading audience, but this may not always be the case since there's the possibility of persons outside of your class and/or the university reading your work.

Some useful things to keep in mind:

- Work within word count limits. In your writing classes (and beyond), your instructors want you to learn how to use language effectively; part of doing so is adhering to word counts. When you write with the clearest and strongest language possible, you create a highly effective piece. Furthermore, you are demonstrating that you clearly are aware of and understand the rhetorical situation.

- In many writing classes, instructors will often use a theme to frame the content (the readings and writings you'll do during the semester). Likewise, blogs may continue that theme. It is important that you address the specific requirements of any assignment you are given as well as adhere to the overarching theme of the blog.

- Blog entries and comments are collaborative: This allows your peers to offer suggestions for editing purposes and other types of ways to expand your writings. It is a good idea to consider these suggestions as you think through the writings that the entire class has generated as well as what you've posted. These suggestions are crucial parts of the writing process and writing community of the classroom.

- Although academic blogging is similar in format to personal writing that you may do for your own social networking, blog posts and comments connected with coursework should focus on the topic at hand and be a contribution to the class exploration of the subject. To keep this focus, you should avoid personal tangents and slang comments that are often found in personal digital writing spaces.

Online Discussion Forums

With the growing usage of online e-learning systems such as Moodle, online discussion forums (also known as discussion boards) have become a part of many courses. These are essential to hybrid and online courses, but these forums can also be used in connection with traditional classroom courses since they present opportunities to interact with one another that aren't always possible within the time constraints of a traditional class meeting. Discussion "threads" allow an ongoing conversation on a course-related topic that allows you to present your ideas as well as respond to the ideas of your classmates.

Discussion forums are graded course requirements in most cases, but they differ from typical course writing assignments such as essays and written homework assignments because they require interaction between the class members. Traditional writing assignments are written in response to a prompt, passed in, and revisited only if revision is requested by the instructor or required by a portfolio assessment at the end of a semester; discussion topics in an online forum are meant to foster an interactive discussion of the topic with class participants. Given the format and rhetorical situation, some instructors may choose to read and *respond only when necessary* to allow you as students to work through your ideas and exchange them with one another.

The following strategies are key to creating and participating in constructive online discussions:

- Review the specific guidelines for the assigned discussion forum. Online discussion forums offer a number of options for assignments. Don't assume that discussion assignments will be the same from one class to the next or even from one assignment to the next in the same course. Reading, posting, and responding are frequent requirements. Make sure you understand what is expected from you in each of these areas.

- Submit your posts by the deadline(s) set by your instructor. Some courses may include *staggered* deadlines. This means you may be required to post your initial response to the prompt by one date and responses to other students' posts by a later date. If the forum has one set deadline for posts and responses (instead of *staggered* deadlines), you need to set your own deadline for posting. If you wait until right before the deadline to submit your initial response post, you will not give your fellow students a reasonable amount of time to read your post. This may result in little or no responses to your post, which can result in reduced interaction with your fellow classmates and, in some cases, a lessening of your grade for the assignment.

- Read the posts and responses of your peers. While you need to read (and respond as necessary) to responses left to your initial post, you also want to read the initial posts of your fellow classmates as well as responses to their posts. This allows you the opportunity to compare ideas and create constructive discussions that incorporate various viewpoints. If you are only reading responses to your initial post, you are focusing only on your own ideas and not interacting with the ideas of others.

- Interact with the discussions in the forum. When you respond to the posts of classmates, address the content, not style (unless this is specifically required by the assignment) of the posts. Forums are opportunities to carry on a continuous conversation on a topic, but this is dependent upon the quality of the responses submitted to main posts. Just like traditional in-class peer feedback and/or response sessions, a comment such as "Good post" or "I agree" leads to no further discussion. As a part of a scholarly community, you should offer more substantial comments (often your instructor will have a length in mind) that interact with the content of your peers' posts.

Writing Rhetorically in Digital Spaces

Inventing throughout the Writing Process

Michelle Cox and Anne Doyle

We often think of invention–the creation of new ideas and text–as taking place during brain-storming, but it happens throughout the writing process. We also often think of invention as a solitary act, happening solely in the mind of the writer, but, in fact, invention often happens socially, while in conversation with others or in response to reader feedback. In other words, invention can happen rhetorically, in relation to purpose and audience. In this section, we will explore strategies that can be used at different points in the writing process either by writers working individually or in collaboration with a partner or writing group.

Strategies to Use toward the Beginning of the Writing Process

The most important element of topic selection is finding a topic you really feel strongly about, one that you truly want to explore or communicate about to an audience. Of course, in college writing you will sometimes be asked to write on a specific topic; on those occasions, you will need to discover the elements of this topic which you want to explore or about which you feel strongly.

As you read through these strategies, and as you idea-generate and begin to assemble your ideas, remember that most topics–even apparently straightforward and simple ones–have lay-ers of complexity which you can discover and exploit in your writing.

1. **Listing:** This strategy is useful at the very beginning of the process when starting a writing project where you have open topic choice. First, divide a page into six columns. At the top of each column, write "People," "Places," "Events," "Controversies," "Memories," and a title of your choosing. Then, in each column, list as many topics as you can think of within ten minutes. Then, circle the three topics that seem most interesting and freewrite about each of these, testing each topic as a possible choice. You may want to sketch out ideas for how you might explore this topic or list questions that this topic raises for you. Think of these freewrites as opportunities to test drive the topic before making your final selection. Then, meet with a partner or writing group to get feedback on your ideas.

2. **Clustering or Webbing:** This strategy, which may be familiar to you from high school, could be used in conjunction with listing or as a separate strategy. Once you find a topic that seems generative, you can either cluster or web to brainstorm additional words, ideas,

or questions you associate with this topic. To cluster, write down the topic and then free-associate, seeing where the topic leads you. To web, write down the topic in the center of a piece of paper and then draw branches out from the topic, associating along different lines for each branch. Then, meet with a partner or writing group to get feedback on your ideas.

3. **Question Generator:** This strategy may be more useful for research projects. On a piece of notebook paper, write down your topic and three researchable questions you want to answer related to this topic. Then, round robin this piece of paper with either a writing group or with the entire class, passing your topic and questions to a student to your right. When you receive another student's topic and questions, star the question that seems most interesting to you, add another researchable question, and pass it along to a student to your right. When you add a question, think about how you can help the writer push forward his/her thinking as well as what you feel readers would want to know about this topic. Continue until each topic receives feedback from at least three students.

4. **Questions from the Audience:** This strategy is similar to the above, but is a bit more involved, and more useful once you have completed some preliminary research. On top of a large piece of paper, use a marker to write your main research question. Under this, summarize why you chose this question and what you already know about this topic. Then list research questions that extend your main research question, making sure to leave some room at the bottom for responses. Tape your poster on the wall of your classroom. Once everyone's posters are hung, walk around the classroom. Stop at posters that pique your interest (or do not have many student responses) and do the following: read through the poster, place a star next to the question you find most interesting (this may be one of the writer's questions or a question added by another student), and then add a question of your own. When you add a question, think about how you can help the writer push forward his/her thinking as well as what you feel readers would want to know about this topic.

Strategies to Use Somewhere in the Middle of the Writing Process

Writers continue to think of new ideas and make new connections in the midst of the writing process, both during the creation of the first draft and between drafts. In fact, our minds are most free to continue thinking after the hard work of writing the first draft is completed and there's time to reflect on what has been written. The following strategies may be useful for continuing invention during the writing process.

5. **Freewriting in the Middle:** Sometimes, we can feel stuck after writing a first draft. We may know that the first draft isn't representative of our thinking or the voice we are aiming for, but we don't know how to move from it. In this case, one of the best strategies is to put that draft away and freewrite. If you are working on a computer, save and close the first draft, and open a new document, entitling it "Freewriting in the Middle." Then, simply freewrite, without worrying about form or sound. Push your thinking forward, experiment with voice. It may also be helpful at this point to return to earlier brainstorms to see if there's something useful in your original thinking that is worth exploring in this

space between drafts. Then, put this draft beside your first draft to see if there's material here worth integrating. Some writers even find that they like the tone or approach in the freewrite more than their first draft and use it as the base for their second draft.

6. **Chat It Out:** This strategy, which has been developed by Panteha Sanati here at Bridgewater State University, makes use of the additional questions of an audience to push a writer's ideas forward. In this approach, you begin by outlining or drafting the narrative, description, or argument you are contemplating; then you "chat it out" with a couple of classmates. These classmates listen and ask questions about the narrative, description, or argument, while they also compare what you are saying with the outline or draft you have written. They then let you know what additional information or reorganizing you did while interacting on the topic with a live audience. In turn, you can take these observations and the questions they had about your material and use these for another brainstorming and organizing session. The advantage of having a live audience is that you hear yourself *map out your paper*, and that your peers can provide immediate feedback. By chatting it out, you have a less abstract sense of your audience, and your peers' comments can help hone your paper's direction, dimension, chronology, and descriptive power.

7. **Looping:** This strategy is useful for further developing a particular area of a draft. Find a line that calls out to you as worth exploring more deeply, copy and paste it to the top of a new document (or write it at the top of a piece of paper) and freewrite from it. This strategy may yield material worth integrating into the draft, yield a new paragraph, or even yield a new direction for the focus of the paper.

8. **Finding Your Voice Again:** During a research project, it is easy to lose your voice in the midst of voices from sources. Here's a series of writing prompts you might find useful after you have completed your research. First, read through your research notes and materials, then, freewrite to the following: Overall, what have you learned from your research? What people, facts, events, or stories stand out as most memorable from your research? Picture yourself in conversation with someone about your research. What questions would they ask? How would you answer? Write down both parts of this dialogue. And, finally, what do you most want to communicate to your audience about your topic? Once you are finished, talk through these freewrites with a partner or writing group.

9. **Counter-arguing:** Argumentative writing is most persuasive when the reader feels that the writer is knowledgeable about and has considered a range of perspectives on the issue, but still chooses to take a particular stance. This strategy is useful in learning what a critical reader may think about when reading your argument. Find a partner and comb through each other's essays, looking for claims that a reader may question or doubt. Then, step into the shoes of a reader that holds a different stance from the writer and ask the writer questions, showing the writer where he/she may want to address counter-arguments, and then ask your partner to do the same for you. Incorporating these counter-arguments may raise your credibility in the eyes of your readers.

10. **Through Another's Eyes:** Here is another strategy useful for gaining insight into another perspective when writing an argumentative or persuasive essay. For about ten minutes, freewrite, sketching out the reasons why an intelligent person would take a stance differing from your own. Think seriously about this, including credible claims, evidence, and alternative perspectives on the issue. Writing from another's point of view on the topic will help you step into their shoes, challenging you to think about the complexity of the issue at hand. Once you've finished this freewrite, return to your draft, and reconsider each claim from this new perspective. You may find that you need to qualify some of the claims or acknowledge other stances on the issue. Some students who have done this exercise have discovered that they weren't as sure about their stances as they thought, and even decided to reframe the argument from a different perspective.

Strategies to Use near the End of the Writing Process

Sometimes, our best ideas come toward the end of the writing process, once we have had a chance to reflect on what we have written, on the choices we have made during the writing process, and on feedback from readers. The following prompts may be useful to you as you finalize a piece of writing.

11. **Do I Really Mean It?** Read through your essay, with a critical eye, testing each idea you put forth. Do you still agree? Revise areas that no longer match up with what you are thinking now.

12. **Where Am I in this Researched Essay?** Read through your essay and underline all summaries, paraphrases, and direct quotes. Then highlight the remaining text. How present is your voice in this essay? If you find that your voice is being squeezed out by the sources, try "looping" to one of your quotations, generating your own language to interpret the significance of this quotation. This strategy may help you integrate more of your voice into your essay.

13. **So What?** Envision a reader saying, "So what?" after reading your essay (or use a writing group meeting to pose this question to each other). How would you answer this question? How would you explain the main point, the overall relevance of your essay? How would you revise to make this significance more obvious to the reader?

14. **Finding Your Thesis:** Often while we write, our ideas change, as writing itself is a tool for learning and thinking. If we don't revise to incorporate these changes in thinking, the introduction and thesis can contain our least clear thinking and seem poorly matched to our conclusions. Read your second to last paragraph and conclusion. Is there a sentence here that would work better as your thesis? If so, revise your introduction, including this new thesis and then rework the end of your essay to push your thinking forward even more.

Prompts #1, 4, and 8 were inspired by Bruce Ballenger's *The Curious Writer* 2nd ed. Pearson-Longman: New York, 2007.

Playing with Revision

Michelle Cox and Katherine E. Tirabassi

You need to get some writing down on paper and to keep it there long enough so that you can give yourself the treat of rewriting. What you need is a ballpoint pen so that you can't erase and some cheap paper so you can deliberately use a lot of it . . . Where are your notes to yourself? Where are your lists? . . . Where are your quoted passages? Where is your chaos? Nothing comes of nothing!

Ann Berthoff, "Recognition, Representation and Revision"

Revision is the time when you are free to play with language, experiment with form and voice, and explore your ideas and memories more deeply. The following prompts were developed to help guide you in revision, providing multiple ideas for further developing content, organization, and style.

The prompts listed under "Developing the Meaning" and "Style and Eloquence" are useful when revising a wide range of texts, from researched essays, to letters to the editor, to creative non-fiction. You may find the prompts listed under "Playing with Time" and "Layering in the Details" most useful when revising works of creative non-fiction.

Developing the Meaning

1. **Finding the Focus:** Does your essay feel unwieldly, scattered? Read through the essay and circle the part that most clearly zones in on what you want to write about or hints at an insight you experienced while writing. In the rest of the piece, underline the phrases that need to be in the next draft. Now, rewrite, starting as close to the circled part as you can, and ending soon after the circled part ends. You may find that this new writing leads to a whole new draft, or you may choose to incorporate this writing into your existing draft.

2. **Do You Really Mean It?** Revision gives the opportunity to reflect on and further develop your ideas. Read over your draft, and ask yourself if you still believe or agree with everything you wrote. Write reflective notes in the margins as you read, and then revise, while referring to these notes.

3. **Talk about Your Writing:** Ask someone to read your writing who is willing to talk with you seriously about what you've written. During this conversation, note what your reader asks questions about, finds interesting, wants to know more about. When you revise, picture this reader as your audience.

4. **Looping:** Look through your draft and identify a line that calls out to you, one that seems to hold meaning. Take out a new piece of paper, copy this line at the top, and freewrite from it, pushing to further develop meaning as you go. Look over this new writing, identify another line that calls out to you, and repeat the process.

Style and Eloquence

5. **Activate Your Verbs**: There are going to be situations when passive voice is preferable, such as when you are writing for scientific audiences or in cases when you want to deemphasize the subject. However, active verbs are often more direct than passive verbs. A test you can use to distinguish between active and passive voice is to try adding a "by . . ." phrase to the sentence. If you can add a "by . . ." phrase, the sentence uses passive voice. For example: Active: *Karen made the cookies.* Passive: *The cookies were made by Karen.* The second example is passive, because a "by . . ." phrase is added: *The cookies were made by Karen.* One more tip: Using too many "ing" verbs can slow down the pace of your prose. For example, instead of *I was running*, use *I ran*. Save "ing" verbs for times when you want to slow the action in a scene, such as describing the moment before an accident occurred or watching a leaf falling to the ground.

6. **Cut, Cut, Cut:** Comb through your essay and cut as much as you possibly can. Try for fifteen words per page. Cut extra words that don't add meaning, such as "really," "very," "basically," "thing," "it," "it was," "it is," "there were," "there is," "this is," and "that." Example: *My brother's constant whining is one of those many characteristics that really frustrates me to no end* can be cut to *My brother's constant whining frustrates me.* Cut wordy phrases that don't add meaning, such as *on the other hand, due to the fact that, needless to say, in my personal opinion, at this point in time.* Cut redundant words, such as "big tall skyscraper." The words "big" and "tall" have similar meanings, and using the specific word "skyscraper" tells your reader that the building you're referring to is a large building.

7. **Sentence Variety:** Readers appreciate a change of pace, and varying sentence lengths and structure can add that sense of texture to your writing, and help you better emphasize key pieces of information. Comb through your draft and focus in on your sentences. Count the number of words in each sentence. How many sentences are the same length? Look at the structure of your sentences. How many include introductory phrases, conjunctions, or dependant clauses? Read your essay out loud, listening to the rhythm, noting places where you stumble over a word or strive to emphasize something that's not being emphasized by the writing. Then revise, using short sentences for emphasis, long sentences for depth and description, moving important pieces of information to the ends of sentences for added emphasis.

8. **Focusing on Pronouns:** Here are some strategies for tightening your writing in relation to pronoun use: Comb through your draft and circle all instances of "it." The phrase "it is" at the beginning of a sentence (It is a quiet, gentle rain) can be used for emphasis, but overuse waters down this emphasis. Other uses of "it" can make writing sound vague. "There" at the beginning of the sentence can have the same effect. Try replacing "it" and "there" with more specific words. Now circle all uses of the words "this" and "these." Many times, when "this" or "these" is not followed by the word the pronoun is referring to, the writing can sound vague and foggy (e.g., This is long and cumbersome versus This sentence is long and cumbersome). Then, circle all uses of "he," "she," "you," "we," "they," etc. Make sure each pronoun has a clear referent, a particular person that the pronoun refers to.

Playing with Time

9. **Flashback:** Narratives don't need to follow a strict timeline starting at the beginning and detailing each chronological event to the end. In fact, doing so can drag out your story, compelling you to include details and events that are not essential to your main point. Try mixing it up by using a strategy like flashback, which allows you to move back and forth in time and only include the details and events that are significant. One thing to watch out for: make sure you make the shift in time clear to your reader, using signals such as changes in verb tense (present tense to past tense), white space surrounding the flashback, and the return to specific details that ground the reader in the framing story.

10. **Time Stretch:** Psychological time operates very differently from clock time. Sometimes an incident that only took a few minutes holds a great deal of significance. Look for an incident like this in your narrative, and write a page or more about it. Recall those few minutes in detail. Replay them in slow motion. Try to use at least three of the five senses.

11. **Time Summary:** Time summaries are useful when you want to indicate to the reader quickly that a long period of time has passed or to indicate the repetition and similarity of events, such as when you want to describe a typical day at the office or what usually happens at family reunions. To use this technique, compress a long period of time into a paragraph. Let readers know the length of time you are summarizing. Words like "often," "frequently," "always," "usually," "again and again," "sometimes," and especially "would" suggest that actions are repeated. Here's an example of a time summary: *Summers at the Cape always started like this. The long wait to cross the Bourne Bridge, while my sister and I talked about all that we would do that summer in Sandwich. The thrill of unlocking the cottage door and running through the rooms, making sure nothing had changed. The rush of visiting our favorite haunts again–the Boardwalk, Pizzas by Evan, Mary's Bookstore. But then reality would set in Monday morning when Dad left to work in Worcester for the week, and we'd remember the long weeks of boredom, without Dad, without familiar neighbors, without friends from school.*

Layering in the Details

12. **Describe a Person:** Choose a person relevant to your essay's focus and describe all physical features, dress, smell, mannerisms, how he/she talks, how he/she interacts with people, so that your reader would be able to identify this person in a crowded room.

13. **Describe a Place:** Fully describe a specific location relevant to your essay's focus. Describe everything you see, smell, hear, taste, feel. Bring the reader right into your experience of this place.

14. **Describe an Object:** Choose a significant object that you mention in your essay, and fully describe it, referring to all of your senses. For example, if you mention a journal, show the cracks in the journal binding, the frayed edges of the fabric, the way your handwriting looks messy and excited at some places, and relaxed and contemplative in other places.

15. **Take Another Look:** Return to a place or dig out an object that you mention in your essay. Write about new details that you notice or new memories that arise.

16. **Talk to Someone Who Knows:** Informally interview a person who is important to the events you discuss in one of your pieces. Ask this person questions to fill gaps in your memory. Insert what you learn into your essay.

17. **Unbury a Story:** Find a line in your essay that seems to hide a story, and unbury that story. You might find a line that "tells" but doesn't "show." Open up that story. Belief statements, such as "I can't write," often hold one or more stories within them. Choose one of these stories to tell.

18. **Add, Add, Add:** Comb through your essay and add details that help your audience better understand what you see and mean when you use certain words. Change vague nouns (*car*) to specific nouns (*Nissan Quest*), general adjectives (*red*) to specific ones (*metallic cherry*), direct statements (*my minivan handles well*) to metaphors (*When shifting across three lanes to get to my exit, my minivan handles like what I imagine a racecar to feel like, hugging the road while cleanly gliding to the next lane, and responding quickly to my every move*).

Prompts #5, 6, 7, 9, 10, 11 are inspired by Rebecca Rule and Susan Wheeler's *True Stories: Guides for Writing from Your Life*. Porsmouth, NH: Heinemann, 2000.

Peer Review in College-Level Writing

Daniel Johnson

Peer review is a process in which writers give feedback on each other's work. As a self-regulating device, all disciplines use peer review in one form or another. When academics publish in professional journals, a panel of scholars from the same field evaluates their work in order to ensure the quality of the journal. The rate of acceptance is typically low, but every author receives suggestions on what could be done to improve his or her work. But for the majority of scholars, peer review begins much earlier: we write and revise and ask our colleagues to read and critique, all with an eye toward helping us improve our writing.

In college, you will engage in peer review sessions with other students where you will exchange papers to read and provide an outside perspective on each other's writing. The difference between professional peer reviewing and college peer reviewing is that in college you will most likely be face to face in the same room with the author of the paper you provide comments on. Your instructor will also provide you with some guidelines as to what you need to achieve at the end of your peer-review session.

These sessions will help you develop an awareness of what makes a good paper and what may hinder it. Reading and discussing your peers' work will require patience, an eye for detail, and the ability to tactfully give constructive criticism. Listening to your peers discuss your draft will enhance your awareness of how your writing effects an audience other than yourself and your instructor.

It is important to remember that peer reviewing is a skill, and as a student you will have to continuously work at becoming a better reader and writer of your own and others' work.

There will never be a paper that we write that cannot undergo some sort of revision, large or small, and conducting peer review sessions will help you identify elements of writing that needs more development as well as celebrate what you and other writers have done well.

There will be many questions that you will have about the practical side of reading and commenting on your own and others' work, but, at the very least, what you need to keep in mind is that the goal of peer review is to get a clear picture of how to improve our writing and express our exact meaning in the appropriate voice for the assignment. Another point to consider is that peer review is a not a venue to make new friends. That said, it doesn't mean that you can't be friendly with other students, and you should, but the objective of peer review is to receive enough suggestions to craft an even better paper and to be able to make helpful comments on the work of others. So while smiley faces, stars, and comments like "cute!" might have been appropriate for high school, they will not add substance to either your or other students' collective knowledge of honing a finely crafted paper.

Conversely, being negative about someone else's writing, dismissing it all together or paying attention exclusively to grammatical mistakes or other mechanical errors, will not result in a productive peer review exchange. Try to focus on developing a balance so that you and your peers comment on the overall content and structure of the paper, rhetorical devices used by the writer, the depth and originality of thinking as well as the clarity of expression. Comments on the mechanics of writing, including grammar and punctuation are definitely helpful but can be reserved for the second or third round of your peer review. Remember the goal of peer review is not to evaluate a finished product, but to provide feedback on how to revise and edit. In most cases, it is helpful to go through several peer-review sessions, with each one focusing on a specific set of goals and concerns.

Below are a few guidelines created to help you set up a basic peer-review session. This is by no means inclusive, and your instructor will have additional suggestions tailored to the specific of a particular assignment. As you become more engaged and familiar with peer review, you will also develop your own approach to this important stage in the writing process.

Guidelines for a Basic Peer Review Session

You will be working with another student in the class. Exchange your papers and read your partner's paper carefully. As you are reading, be aware of your reaction as a reader. Use your pen or pencil to mark both examples of writing that you like and the errors or inconsistencies that you notice. Please be considerate and use constructive criticism. Use the questions below to help you started.

1. What is the main idea of the essay? Can you highlight the thesis? Does it need any clarification? If there is no thesis, can you attempt to state it in your own words?

2. What did you like about the essay? Feel free to highlight the passages that you enjoyed reading. What attracted you to these passages? Do you have any suggestions as to how the writer can improve them?

3. Have you found any redundancies or points that do not support the writer's main idea? Please highlight them in the draft and make suggestions on what can be done to avoid these problems.

4. What type of evidence does the writer use to facilitate your understanding of the writer's main point? What information would you suggest to add or to omit?

5. Read over the conclusion and consider if the writer is able to bring the paper to a close, which satisfies you as a reader. How relatable is the essay to you? Do you have any questions to the writer that have not been answered in the essay?

6. Have you noticed any errors in grammar, word choice, punctuation, and/or spelling? Are there any errors that occur more than once? Please highlight them in the essay and point them out to your partner. What resources can you and your partner use to address these concerns?

Contemplative Practices and English as a Second Language Learning

Julia Stakhnevich

Second language learning is a lifelong process that requires a certain measure of courage to go beyond the immediate comfort zone of the first language. It also benefits from introspection, or the ability to monitor what we do as language learners and how what we do impacts our communication in the language and culture that we study. It is through contemplative practice that we could become more aware both of our strengths and challenges as English language learners and writers. This self-awareness is a critical step in achieving a higher level of language proficiency.

The first step toward a better understanding of who we are as language learners might be to recognize the efforts that we have put into noticing new language material around us: Whenever we open a book, engage in a conversation, prepare a presentation, and write a paper, there is always a potential to encounter new words and expressions, to uncover new ways of using specific language structures, and to become more perceptive to the cultural values and assumptions transmitted through the rhetoric of the second language. We need to cultivate our curiosity and channel it into a productive language learning process. Seeing the unknown as an opportunity to learn could help alleviate the stress and anxiety that might arise as part of the experience of learning another language.

As language learners, we are attuned toward noticing differences between languages and cultures. While sometimes these differences might be surprising, they might also add a new dimension to our understanding of the first language and culture. For us to be successful in the new sociolinguistic environment, we need to find ways to feel comfortable and secure when encountering unavoidable ambiguities inherent in language study and culture crossing. One way of achieving this goal is to acknowledge our own active role in cross-cultural exchanges and language learning. This will allow us to take control of the learning process, become more active, and connect to our emotional responses to various language learning situations.

Finally, although language learning might not be easy, we need to approach it with a sense of playfulness and enjoyment, the qualities that will help us sustain interest in the process of becoming more proficient speakers and writers in the second language. Below are several writing prompts that might inspire you to become a more introspective language learner:

1. What ideas/associations come to mind when you think about the work that you have done to master this language? What worked for you in the past? What is working for you now? How was/is it different to use English for oral communication as opposed to writing in English?

2. We can use language for communication and as our thinking tool. Reflect on how you feel when you have to use English as your main tool of communication. Consider how it makes you feel to rely on English to express your deep thoughts in writing.

3. Bilinguals often code-switch: insert words or phrases from one language in the discourse of another. In which situations do you think this would be an effective communication strategy? Will it ever be possible in writing? How would it make you feel to be able to incorporate both languages in your writing process? What creative strategies might you use to be able to do it successfully? What could you do to help your audience appreciate your writing style?

Benefits of Journaling in a Second Language

Julia Stakhnevich

Reflection is one of the key strategies that second language writers can utilize to enhance their writing knowledge in English. By consciously considering strengths and challenges in their writing, second language writers can develop effective approaches to address both. A language journal is an excellent vehicle for self-reflection that offers a space to practice writing without being judged by others, to develop fluency as a writer, and to explore complex ideas related to writing and language usage in general.

Each writer can decide on their own on the topics that they would like to explore in the journal. It is also a matter of personal choice how often they would like to write in it: some writers prefer to comment on particular daily events, others choose to write from time to time. What is important is to be persistent and continue keeping a journal even in the context of a busy schedule at school or at work. Writing for as little as five or ten minutes on a regular basis can make a difference.

Journaling to Reflect on Writing

Regardless of how often writers journal, the journal becomes a private repository for ideas about how they currently approach writing in English and what they can do to improve their writing style now and in the future. For example, writers may consider their current achievements in writing. How much progress have they made since the year before, since taking the last language course, or since being enrolled in a writing class? What are the specific moments, scenes, situations, and/or people (teachers, friends, family, strangers) that have made an impact on how they write in English? What are the writers' favorite writing assignments? Why? What kind of texts do they like to read in English? What kind of texts do they like to read in their first language?

Journaling to Express Emotions

With a language journal being a private document, it can be also used as a space to express emotions with regard to reading, writing, and speaking in English. To do this more vividly, writers might consider using figurative language (e.g. metaphors and similes). For example, one can begin a journal entry with "Reading and writing in English is like . . ." or "Speaking in English about myself/my family/school is like . . ." Whatever literary devices writers choose to include, the point is to stay true to one's emotions and channel them into writing. For many writers, this is an effective way of increasing fluency in writing while sustaining authenticity in the selection of the topics for their writing.

Journaling to Explore the First Language as a Writing Resource

Another topic to explore in a journal is how to use the first language as a resource when writing in a second. For instance, writers might want to consider their knowledge of cognate words, cultural events, traditions, stories learned in their first language and reflect on how this knowledge can be utilized to enhance their writing in English. Are there any connections that writers see between writing in English and writing in their first language? Writers might also want to discuss if and when it is okay to rely on the first language when preparing assignments that will be ultimately presented in English. Another set of topics to reflect upon is the role of the first language in one's academic and private life. How important is it for second language writers to stay connected to their first language? What is the impact of English on how they use their first language now and possibly in the future?

Journaling to Expand Vocabulary

A language journal can also serve as a space to write about cross-cultural differences and similarities and to record new words and expressions that writers encounter in textbooks, lectures, or just by conversing with others in English. Some second language writers might find it helpful to use a step-by-step approach to expanding their vocabulary by first recording the term and then trying to figure out its meaning by analyzing the context in which it was used. The second step might be looking it up in a thesaurus in English. Finally, if necessary, one could turn to a bilingual dictionary. Looking through vocabulary notes on a regular basis will help remember them better.

Journaling to Increase English Grammar Awareness

For some second language writers, journaling can also be a way to analyze differences and similarities in English grammar and in the grammar of their first language. Writers could look at their own writing samples that have already been corrected by a professor or a tutor. Are there any frequently occurring patterns? Are there any transfer errors from the first language? In other words, are there some instances of relying on the grammar of the first language when writing in the second? Writers may find it helpful to compile lists of these errors and use them as self-checklists when editing their papers.

Journaling to Record Questions about Language and Culture

Journaling can also serve as an effective tool to record one's questions about the English language and how it is used in writing and speech of others, such as questions about new vocabulary, difficult grammar points, surprising rhetorical moves, and/or cross-cultural differences and similarities. Second language writers might then consider bringing their journals to their meetings with ESL tutors, conversation partners, Writing Studio consultants, and/or professors. Journal entries that contain questions about the language and culture often become an excellent starting point for tutoring sessions and offer second language writers an active role in shaping their interactions with tutors and instructors.

Whether journaling is used as an editing tool, a repository for ideas, an emotional outlet, a technique to extend one's vocabulary, a communication tool between the writer and a tutor or professor, or a way to reflect upon the writer's language use in general, experience shows that it is an effective strategy to promote fluency in writing and to achieve a better understanding of what it takes to write effectively in a second language.

Embracing Writing
Awards for Writing Excellence

Embracing Writing holds an annual competition to recognize excellent writing in ENGL 101, ENGL 102, First Year Seminar, and Second Year Seminar. Students who submit excellent work in the below categories may have it published in the next edition of *Embracing Writing*.

The winner of each of the following categories will receive $50 and be guaranteed publication, and will be recognized at the Embracing Writing **Awards Reception in the fall:**

1. *Excellence in Creative Non-Fiction*–Awarded to a student essay written for ENGL 101 or ENGL 102 that demonstrates insight and effective use of voice and other literary devices.

2. *Excellence in Persuasive Writing*–Awarded to a student paper written for ENGL 101 or ENGL 102 that demonstrates effective use of illustration or evidence to support a thesis, using an appropriate citation format to cite sources, if used.

3. *Excellence in Researched Writing*–Awarded to a student essay written for ENGL 101 or ENGL 102 that demonstrates effective use of secondary sources to support an argument or inform readers, using an appropriate citation format.

4. *Excellence in First Year Seminar Writing*–Given to a student for an exemplary paper, written in First Year Seminar, that serves to reinforce, share, or interpret knowledge, and makes excellent use of supporting evidence.

5. *Excellence in Second Year Seminar Writing*–Given to a student for an exemplary paper, written in Second Year Seminar, that serves to reinforce, share, or interpret knowledge in a specific academic discipline.

6. *Excellence in Writing on the Topic of Sustainability*–Given to a first or second year student for an exemplary essay, written in a 100- or 200-level course, that serves to reinforce, share, or interpret knowledge related to sustainability, and includes the three key areas of sustainability: environment, economy, and social justice.

7. Excellence in Writing Quantitative Argument–Given to a first or second year student for an exemplary essay written in a 100- or 200-level course, in which numerical or statistical reasoning is a central theme to the argument.

Electronic submissions are accepted during both fall and spring semesters; all submissions are due by 5 pm on the last class day of spring semester. Students are welcome to submit multiple papers, but each essay should be submitted for only one category. If the editors feel that the submission is noteworthy for another category, they will consider it for that category's award.

For each submission, please complete the submission form, which can be found at http://www.bridgew.edu/WAC/WritingAtBSU/StudentPublicationVenues.cfm. Email the submission form and your submission to Dr. Julia Stakhnevich.

Award-Winning Essays

To give you a sense of the kinds of writing being produced in Writing I and II and in First and Second Year Seminars, *Embracing Writing* includes a number of sample essays by students at Bridgewater State University.

Creative Non-Fiction

Matthew Griffin

A Silent Rebirth

2013 Award for Excellence in Creative Non-Fiction

This work of creative non-fiction examines how one tragic event can change a person's life. To accomplish this, the narrator speaks in both the first and third person. The first person "I," the third person "he," and the third person "Matt" all refer to the same individual. He is looking at the moment he hears the news as well as previous times leading up to the event (in italics) to try to get an understanding of who he was and who he is now that he has experienced this loss. The shift in pronouns indicates the identity confusion, inner conflict, and coping mechanisms triggered by this event. Such shifts are sometimes used in creative pieces but are not generally appropriate for other academic writing because they bring attention to the style as much as the content of the piece. For the reader, such changes can either add dimension to the piece by leaving the reader as unsettled as the narrator, or they can be confusing and jarring. As you read the essay, consider how the shifting perspectives impact your reading. Does it add to the emotional impact of the piece or does it add unnecessary confusion?

The sound of her voice filled my ear, but for some reason I couldn't fully grasp the words. The slight sobs echoed through my mind. Pounding away, until the words came into focus. She was telling me the one thing I did not want to hear, the one thing I had been sure would not happen, the one thing that would change so much about the life I knew. Silence ran throughout the room and breathed down my neck. She no longer spoke and neither did I. With a tear streaming down my face, the phone went dead. I then allowed myself to fall apart and shatter against my bedroom floor, and still the ring of silence filled the room, for my throat had closed and no noise could escape.

He was a boy once. Although he felt as if those days were now long ago. Everyone was a kid at one point in his or her life; it's how we all start. The transition from childhood to adulthood is so fast that it's hard to even notice there even was a transformation. Humans are amazing in the way that they all see everything in a different way. Things use to fascinate him. From the brick red crayon he always went for first, to a single golden, crisp leaf left on a tree in the fall breeze. He asked questions. A three-hour car ride was easily filled with his voice yelling over the radio and sounds of the highway. He had family, with whom he spent as much time as he could. Above all though, he had friends. Although some came and went, every child has friends, and so did he.

His name was Matt, and when he was young he knew who he was. Most kids can't say that at seven years old, but he could. He knew he was a happy kid with goals, dreams, and wishes. He loved everything about being young and all the adventures it held: from camping trips, to fighting off monsters, and of course being invincible. His biggest dream, though, was to grow up. He wanted to know how it felt to read the morning paper, drink coffee, and ramble on about words he didn't understand such as mortgage and bills. How was he to know that there was so much more to adulthood?

Days went by and seasons changed. He grew older and older and watched as each year brought on a new challenge and a new chance at growing up and being an adult. The day came when he went to high school. This was something he could not wait for. At this moment, he was grown up (at least in his eyes). Still knowing who he was, he held his head high and walked down the halls, although he was not too sure where he was going yet. With age he gained knowledge and responsibility. He knew that wherever he went, though, he had friends at his side, and that was most important to him. He had his best friends whom he loved more than anything, but he also had a variety of friends here and there and was always making new ones. One of these friends was a boy named Daniel. Daniel was odd, but Matt liked him. He wasn't widely accepted by others, and I admit, Matt didn't always accept him either. Over time, Daniel grew on Matt, and they became best friends. Months went by and the seasons turned to a cold winter as Daniel and Matt settled into their sophomore year. Things appeared as if they were going well, but I should have known it was all about to go wrong. The way Daniel had begun to act was unnerving. He seemed upset, as if he wasn't himself. When he left that afternoon to get on the bus, he hugged Matt. I felt as if something was so wrong when they said goodbye that day, I just never spoke up enough to warn Matt.

That night the phone rang. It was a familiar ring tone; one he heard every night when his friend Kailey called him to talk about the day. Her voice sounded different, though. Her normal enthusiasm had been replaced by a drained voice that filled Matt with sadness. His heart stopped as her voice cut through the phone and whispered the words he never wanted to hear: Daniel died.

That was the very moment I took over. Matt crashed to the floor and the phone went dead. In this moment, I was born, and like every other child, I entered this world in tears. I had to find the strength to put everything back into place and to pick myself up enough to return a call to Kailey. Through tears, I ask why he would commit suicide and if anything was left behind. Nothing was—just confusion and rumors spreading around. On this day, I became the new Matt. Although I'm not sure who I really am, I know it's my job to keep strong and carry on. To be grateful for all I have and to take nothing, and especially no one, for granted, because one day they may not be there.

This brings me to today, to right now, writing this. Who am I? Am I Matt, or someone completely different? I was a boy once, or at least Matt was. He knew who he was. I, on the other hand, wasn't born until I was fifteen, or should I say reborn. In all death there is a rebirth, where something else must come from the ashes. Within this rebirth a new much stronger man was created. I may have missed out on a childhood, but Matt lived it for me. In return, it's now my job to be an adult and to really know what growing up is. Growing up is not bills and Sunday morning coffee; it is being able to show love toward one another and to be grateful and true. Every day I think of Daniel and how much I miss him, and thank him for all he was and still is, and for helping shape who I have become. I'm not completely sure who I am, but maybe that is how it is meant to be. All I can do is live day to day, smile as much as possible, and love having the people in my life that I do. Someday it will all come together. For now though, I'm just a mystery waiting to be solved.

Jean Kesner Mervius

I Am a Survivor

2012 Award for Excellence in Creative Non-fiction

This entry in the Creative Non-fiction category explores the author's personal narrative in a memoir *style of writing. Through the sharing of experiences, the writer explores larger social issues that impact us all. Some of the areas touched upon include the recent devastating earthquake in Haiti, the issue of social justice across socioeconomic lines, immigration and roadblocks facing new citizens, and the feelings of isolation experienced both by non-native language speakers and adult learners returning to college. The examination of these issues, coupled with the writer's skill in telling his story and his ability to unveil insights, illustrates well the role of self in Creative Non-fiction, as well as the role of* self *in the college experience.*

Readers should observe the author's use of reflection, narrative, and dialogue, but pay careful attention to the repetition of key phrases highlighting each experience and how those phrases create a framework for the piece. As you read, ask yourself how those phrases reinforce specific ideas. How do they reveal the author's perception of self? Does this work of Creative Non-fiction achieve a "transcendental truth" that speaks to readers of all backgrounds? And would this framing of the narrative be something you could adapt to your own writing? What would be its benefits or limitations?

I am what I am. I am Jean Kesner Mervius. I am Haitian.

I have been in the United States since May 10, 2010. Four months after the deadly earthquake killed more than 300,000 compatriots, including some of my family, close friends, and co-workers. I survived thanks to a news report that I went to do for my radio station where I had been working for three years as a Journalist/Reporter. Thirty minutes after I left, the building where the radio station was located collapsed with twenty co-workers inside. They all died. I am what I am. I am a survivor.

Here I am in America. A *"just come"* who had been given a visa to get married in ninety days. Otherwise, I would have gone back into my country destroyed by the earthquake. Go back to live again in a tent like many others without bed, without food, without water, without clothes, etc. I am who I am; the only hope of my family and my friends back in Haiti who believe it is easy to make money in America.

Many other Haitians think the same. Here I am in that country, not authorized to work because I do not have a green card or a work permit. Different from Haiti, America is where you must be qualified to have access to certain things. My fiancée, whom I married weeks later, found me a Social Security Number so that I can work. With a passport about to expire and a Social Security Card, I went into every store in my neighborhood looking for a job. Although I was ready to do any work just to make some money, no manager wanted to hire me because I do not have any work experience in America. How could I have any work experience if no one gives me a chance to start? *Oh! Sorry, that's the way it is in the United States.* You may have been a medical doctor or a lawyer in your country, but once you get into the US you need to start your life over. It doesn't matter who you are or where you're from. By the way, medical doctor and lawyer are the most valuable professions in my country. Almost every parent wants their child to become one of those two respectful professions. I am what I am. I am a survivor.

I am what I am. My primary languages are French and Haitian Creole. In America, I had to learn English to survive. One week after I came, I went to Career Works UMass Donahue Institute in Brockton, close to where I live, to take an English class. I was required to take a test first. The idea was to evaluate my level in English before I start taking classes. The test was about my experience in America. In a couple of hours, I was required to answer a number of questions, such as: What do you think about the American culture? What difference do you see between Haiti culture and United States culture? I felt so embarrassed that day because that was the first time I was asked to say something in English. It was extremely difficult for me to even understand the sense of the questions. Nevertheless, I am "advanced in English," said the woman after the test. *Excuse me, did you say advanced?* Yes, you are advanced. Oh! Yeah! I am advanced in English when I can understand just a few words when someone is talking to me. They put my name on a waiting list for the next semester and gave me a list of websites that can help me improve my English.

Ambitious to learn, I started a week later taking English classes at Harbor One, Multicultural Bank in Brockton. My goal was to speak as a native speaker does. Therefore, I took some extra classes online at *learnamericanenglish.com*. How could a man like me, who came to America when I was 26 years old, be able to speak English as someone who was born here? I do realize so many sacrifices such a goal requires. At the class, I was not afraid to ask questions. I was talkative because I was told that is how you learn, by asking questions. Two months later, my English teacher advised me to leave the class because he said this English level was too low for me. I anticipated a lot in the class by asking so many advanced questions. *"Why don't you go straight to college since you can express yourself?"* he said, and he encouraged me to do so. I am what I am. I am a fast learner.

I wish I came to America earlier. I could have accomplished so many things in my life. Here I am, a man who had to work to pay for my immigration papers. I finally found a job. Thank God! However, two weeks later I had to walk away because my passport was expired. My manager told me that she could not get my name into the system. I could not even get paid for my hours. After taking care of my passport, the first door that had opened to me for work was a fast food restaurant. Five Guys Burger and Fries in Randolph, Massachusetts. I started in the kitchen. Dishes, sweeping, and cleaning were my specific duties until I learned how to cook the fries. From there I moved to the grill, and then the register. I am what I am. I am a cashier.

Saving money to pay for my immigration papers was my priority. Yet, how could I save one thousand dollars when I have bills to pay? I know that you cannot continue to depend on someone when you have a job. I had to take my responsibilities. For once, I could get myself anything with my own money. Unfortunately, the money that I made every week from work was not enough to save. All I could have bought with my paycheck was some clothes and a bus pass to go to work. I am what I am. I am a survivor.

I am what I am. I am not a writer. I had never written a draft before. For a Journalist who was working in radio station, I was mostly speaking, not writing. I was more interested in reading. Reading to have information, to see what's on the news. That's it. When it came to writing, I didn't have any skills. I remember my supervisor at the radio station, who also owns a newspaper, asked me to write an article. It was about an event that had happened close to my house. I was so uncomfortable because I didn't have the writing practice. Afraid to lose my job, I had to write something. Yet, journalist writing is so different. There is no inspiration, no emotions in a journalistic text. It is straight writing. Your job is to give the information without implicating yourself as the writer. I wrote the article anyway. Nevertheless, my supervisor had to cut, change, and remove phrases several times. He even changed the title of the article. See, there is no way I could have been a writer. I am who I am; I didn't like writing.

When I applied to become a student at Bridgewater State University, the Admission Office asked me to write an essay. Since I didn't have either my SAT score or the other documents from my high school, the essay was my only chance to get into BSU. I had to write something, something good, and in English. English! That's not my primary language! Imagine how stressed I was. Running back and forth, not knowing what to say and how to start. My biggest problem was that I had to think in my language first and translate my ideas in English. This process took me some time to find the perfect words in English. I thought I was going to lose this opportunity to go to college. I remembered my English teacher at Harbor One used to tell me that I need to think in English if I want to improve in this language. Even though I speak limited English, I wrote the essay. Since then, I have confidence in myself that I can be a writer. I think a writer is at first someone who has something to say, then finds the better way to say it to make it interesting. I am what I am. I am a survivor.

I am what I am. I am a freshman student at BSU, majoring in Communication Studies. Being a communicator has been always my biggest dream. Being a great speaker, having the communication skills adequate to help me connect to different people and cultures. To learn, understand, change, and exchange for the benefits of the societies. I know it's not going to be easy, considering that I am married and have a son on the way. This means I am going to share myself between my education, my family, and work. However, I am who I am. I am ready to do anything to make my dream comes true. I am optimistic and determined. I am *where* I am, in English Writing Rhetorically class. I am learning to structure my thoughts on paper, to make sense in my drafts, and be a prolific writer. I think I am starting on the right foot.

I am what I am. I will achieve my education. I will graduate. I will make my family proud, my professors and my school.

I am what I am.

I am a survivor.

Daniel Sheehan

The Monsters in the Clouds

2012 Award for Excellence in Creative Non-fiction

While nature can be used to create a peaceful and serene setting in some pieces of writing, this essay shows another side of nature—a relentless, unpredictable, and even destructive side. Through discussion of the various storms experienced by this family, Sheehan shows the development of the main character's own fear concerning these powerful forces. The chronological organization of the essay establishes a basis for the growing dread concerning lightning that culminates in and transforms through the protagonist's personal interaction with a storm.

As you read, consider how the events and emotions of the essay build upon one another. Note how the author uses questions ("When would it come for me?") to demonstrate the doubt and uncertainty that is provoked at the mention of storms. Do you find the use of questions to be effective here? Why or why not? Is this a technique that you would use in your writing? If so, in what kind of situation and for what effect?

Nature can be a very powerful thing. It can be amazing to watch and can make you feel many different emotions. When I was younger, I would sit and watch the Weather Channel with my father just hoping to hear about a thunderstorm. Those were the greatest days growing up, the days when my father and I would sit on the porch and wait to watch the show. Sometimes the storm would fizzle out and we would have waited for nothing, and sometimes we would both cheer as the lightning flashed over and over and the thunder boomed, shaking me in my eight-year-old boots. The street I lived on would flood every time it rained; it turned into a water park. We would drop leaves and then race them as they flowed through the stream. There are very few times that the street was totally covered by water, but on those days, we could sit on the porch for what seemed like hours watching and listening, always counting the seconds to see how long it took to hear the thunder after the flash. This way we could see how far away the storm was; if the counting got shorter, then we knew the show had only just begun.

I watched countless storms during the summer with my father, always learning new things about thunderstorms. I was fascinated with them ever since my dad told me that my uncle had been struck by lightning when he was younger. He was okay since the lightning redirected off a plane, but as he put it, the lightning "fried (his) fingernails off." The more I learned, the more I was afraid. If you can see lightning, or if you can hear the thunder, you are close enough for it to strike you—no matter how far away it seems to be. One strike is ten times hotter than the sun and can melt you inside and out in less than a second. The more I learned, the harder it was to sit on that porch and watch; the lights that seemed at first to be dancing and playing now looked so frightening—like they were monsters just waiting for me to leave the safety of my house so they could fry me like an egg on the sidewalk.

No matter how often my dad would tell me that I was safe, that lightning never struck people in urban areas, I was still terrified to be caught in a storm outside of my house. He told me that it was very rare that lightning ever struck anything that wasn't very high in the air. I started to calm down; I was less afraid, less nervous that the monster would catch me. My fear was dying down until we had one of the biggest storms I had ever seen. My father, brother, and I were out on the porch flinching whenever the monsters whipped around in the sky looking for their next victim. After ten minutes or so of counting how far away the lightning was, the countdown hit zero. As the flash happened, there was an explosion in the house next to us where my grandmother lived. My ears were ringing and my younger brother was crying. Sound ceased to exist as I struggled to lift myself out of my chair for fear that the monster was still out there trying to make us leave the porch so that it could strike again. I ran inside as my father ran to my grandmother's house. She couldn't hear anything out of her left ear and still can't today. The same power of nature that had melted my uncle's fingernails had taken my grandmother's hearing. When would it come for me? Would I be so lucky?

Over the following years, I sat on the porch less and less as I was growing older and did not have the time to sit on the porch as much. I would watch the occasional storm, but none of them ever stood up to the day when it struck so close. I didn't have any interaction with the monster for many years until my worst fear caught up with me.

I was walking to my friend's house across town when the clouds rolled in. I thought nothing of it at first when the rain came pouring down, but when the first flashes started, my nerves caught up with me. I was in the worst place to be, the middle of a school parking lot, so I ran as fast as I could and plastered myself against the wall of the school under the fire escape. I was gasping for air, trying to keep calm, remembering what my dad told me that lighting never strikes in these places, but I couldn't stop the memory of the explosion and my ears ringing and my brother crying and the fear I felt when the monster came for my grandmother. It was here for me now. What could I do? And then the tallest part of the school was struck, and the explosion hit again as I was blinded by the light.

The fear welled up inside me, and I couldn't move, but I didn't even know if I wanted to. Was I safe where I was? Another strike on the top of the school. Lightning was not supposed to strike the same place twice, but there it was again and again trying to break down the school so that it could finally get to me. I stayed flat against those bricks for what seemed like years, praying for the torment to end and for the monster to dwindle into the mist of clouds as I had watched so many times from the safety of my porch. But the storm wouldn't end; the fear wouldn't go away. No matter how many deep breaths I took, it felt like the air

The Monsters in the Clouds

was being stolen from my lungs. I started to choke; I could feel the grip nature had on me getting tighter and tighter as the trees rocked back and forth and the monster slammed against the school. Another flash and the storm was over. The trees calmed and the rain died down slightly. I kept staring at the wall, too frightened to move. After a minute or two, I looked up to see bright-colored clouds. I was safe. I had escaped the monster. Finally, I took the longest breath of relief as the grip loosened and my lungs filled. My greatest fear had caught up to me, but I was safe. I continued walking. Since then I have always taken the time to sit on the porch and watch the lights not out of fear, but respect for what power and fear is locked away in the clouds.

The Monsters in the Clouds

Danielle Scipione

Life's Unexpected Blessings

2011 Award for Excellence in Creative Non-fiction

In this piece of creative non-fiction, the writer uses journalistic style to report on a personal interview she conducted. The essay is especially note-worthy in the ability of the writer to weave together rich descriptions of the interviewee and direct quotations from their conversation, with her own observations and conclusions. One of the challenges of this style of writing is to preserve the authenticity of the interviewee's voice, and the writer succeeds in doing so by interspersing direct quotations with descriptions of what the interviewee is doing or looks like. In other words, as readers we feel the immediacy of the interview and are better able to see the speaker–not only through her words, but also through the descriptions of her actions. As you read this essay, think about what makes it engaging. Do you find the introduction of this essay to be powerful? Why or why not? Is the writer using any strategies that you might consider while writing a paper based on a personal interview?

Sue Linehan watched carefully as Patrick climbed into his tree fort. Being a mother of three, Sue always kept a watchful eye over all her children. She has short blond hair, blue eyes, and a welcoming personality. Although being a work-at-home mom, she has started a disability awareness program at all three elementary schools in the town of Sharon, Massachusetts. Every month, Sue teaches young children about different types of disabilities, such as learning, physical, and mental disabilities. "I love teaching the kids about the many disabilities. You should see their faces light up when they learn how to read Braille or try to maneuver around in a wheelchair," Sue laughingly said. Ever since her middle child, Patrick, was diagnosed with autism, she has been involved in two separate executive committees, for the Family Autism Center in Westwood and for Advocates for Autism: Massachusetts, or AFAM.

Patrick was diagnosed with autism at three. For two years, Sue questioned many of Patrick's strange actions. She wondered why her son played alone, while other children at the nursery played together. Sue could not understand why Patrick had not yet started talking by three, when her first son had started talking at the age of two. Sue was confused about Patrick's tantrums whenever their routine was changed. She was relieved when Patrick was diagnosed because his strange actions now finally had a label.

"This isn't common," she said; "most parents are either depressed or in denial upon first discovering their child has a disability. I at least knew what autism was and knew how to deal with it. Don't get me wrong, I constantly have my ups and downs. I experienced the circle of grieving. There were times when I was resentful, angry, and in denial, but other times when I have hope, acceptance, and gratitude. For instance, watching my oldest son receive his license, graduate high school and go to college were happy but sad times for me. I knew Patrick would never experience any of this and it brought new worries for me." Sue looked down and started rubbing her hands together. She looked up and with tears in her eyes said, "I worry about him, you know. I constantly wonder what will happen when he's finished with school. Will there be adult services? What about a job? How will he support himself? What will happen when his father and I are gone? I never want to put pressure on his siblings about being his sole caretaker, but I do worry."

Sue expressed the joys of having a child with a disability. Her face lit up when she explained how Patrick always sits in the front pew at church and sings along. Everyone loves to see Patrick jump up and down with excitement when the church band plays. Or how Patrick blows kisses at the cashiers at the local supermarket. Everyone in the church, school, and town knows Patrick: "Patrick is quite popular. People will stop us in town just to talk to him." The challenges, obstacles, and experience of raising a child on the autistic spectrum never get boring.

"I remember when Patrick was five. He came downstairs to the living room where his father and I were. He was naked, covered in white primer paint. Head to toe! I quickly called Poison Control in fear of the paint suffocating his pores. His father rushed him upstairs and vigorously scrubbed his body. They must have been in the bathroom for three hours. I don't know what Patrick was thinking–but boy, did he get a good bath out of it!" Sue laughed. "Oh the stories I could tell. I could write a book!"

There are many daily struggles in having a child with a disability. The intensity of the child's disability affects how independent the child can be. Kids with autism like Patrick need constant assistance. For example, Patrick still holds hands with an adult when crossing the street and has all his meals made for him. Parents of disabled children often feel isolated from their family and friends. Even family members sometimes may not understand the child's strange behaviors or routines. Many parents do not have support from their family or social services. These setbacks send many parents into depression and resentment towards the child.

"I have seen this trend in many parents. Since Patrick was young I vowed to myself and my family that I wouldn't let this happen. I go out once a week with friends to de-stress. I also exercise. Walking is a great way to alleviate the stress. I recommend to all new parents to join support groups. It helped me relate with similar problems and taught me how to deal with difficult situations. Don't isolate yourself. It's not healthy for yourself or the child," Sue warned.

Sue has become an advocate for Autism Awareness. She joins local groups, educating the community about autism and similar disabilities. She wants the community to know and understand that autism cannot be cured but should be approached with patience. Through her son Patrick, she teaches others how to be caring and supportive of families with children with autism. Sue herself has started many support groups for parents who feel secluded. Being a parent of a child with autism, she knows the struggles and reaches out to help others who may be experiencing the same thing.

"Having a child with a disability has changed my life for the best," Sue exclaimed. "Patrick taught me patience, patience that I never thought I had. He opened my eyes to the many disabilities and pushed me to my limits. I am so thankful for every day that I get to spend with him because he puts a smile on my face every day. Never turn away from a child who seems to be different, because they just might change your life!"

Persuasive Writing

Yvana Osborne

Celebrity Child's Play: The "Shortcake Strategy" Grown Up

2012 Award for Excellence in Persuasive Writing

This essay discusses the "Shortcake Strategy," a popular advertising technique, used to convince consumers to buy a variety of products. The author details how advertisements trigger viewer familiarity (often, as the writer argues, due to near-total immersion and pop culture) with celebrities in order to get consumers to purchase soda, makeup, toys, and more. Beginning with a first-person anecdote and then transitioning into the use of second-person "you," the author describes a series of celebrity-endorsed product examples (real and imagined). The essay then shifts to third-person and provides a historical background of the Shortcake Strategy and its contemporary applications. The author quotes and cites several sources that discuss this particular method (as well as other marketing techniques). Finally, the essay concludes by offering that while consumers are savvy enough to realize that none of the products will ever make them like celebrities, they "still buy into it." Given what the writer's description of the strategy and the series of examples provided, is the argument about celebrity influence convincing? Is the technique of using "you" effective enough to convince readers that they too might be influenced by such marketing techniques?

During a commercial break, I hear a familiar voice talking on my television. I glance up to notice a familiar face. Immediately I am more interested in the scenario on my TV screen. Not only because I want to know what happens next, but because this face has been on my TV many times before. The familiar man stands in a recording booth and stops for a moment, only to grab a conveniently placed bottle of Sprite. He cracks open the bottle: The sound of the fizzing soda makes my mouth water. One sip of the Sprite instantly empowers him. The clear sparkling soda is shown flowing through his body somehow making him a better performer. The music starts as he enthusiastically utters his popular lyrics: "Last name Ever, first name Greatest!" I sit on my couch in temporary awe as the commercial ends with the image of a Sprite bottle gloriously floating in the middle of my screen. I now sit with the beginnings of a craving for lemon-lime soda and the urge to download Drake's album. Yes, this commercial was a good way to advertise Sprite and his new music, but how and why was it so effective? Using a celebrity, like Drake, is the perfect way to catch the attention of consumers, especially those in my generation.

Some say that vendors target younger consumers such as myself by attaching them to their favorite characters and television shows, then putting out products that relate to these characters, knowing the young viewers will buy. Whether you realize it or not, Drake, has been in the entertainment business for a long time. I remember seeing commercials, and without my parents knowing, sneaking a peak at episodes of *Degrassi*. A young Aubrey Graham, who is now known as Drake, was gracing my television as a new actor. Short clips of him and the other actors behind the scenes showed their everyday lives and made viewers, like me, feel that they knew these teenaged celebrities personally. It's understandable that someone my age is captivated when a celebrity as successful as Drake is supporting a product like Sprite or releasing a new album. Like supporting an old friend, people who have watched Mr. Graham from the time he was sixteen will take an interest in what he is advertising. This method is technically known as the "Shortcake Strategy." Thousands of girls buying Hannah Montana dolls and wearing t-shirts with Miley Cyrus' face plastered on them is the perfect example of this. But what most people don't realize is that this same method is being used to influence buyers of all ages, not just my contemporaries. Companies and advertisers treat adults like children, making sure they feel emotionally attached to their favorite celebrities before trying to sell them anything, which usually results in them buying anything that these celebrities endorse. The best salesman is one who can get the buyer to trust them.

Many consumers may say this isn't true. They say they are too mature and are not affected by advertisements. But, these same naysayers have most likely seen a movie because their favorite actor was in it, or have bought an album because they have been listening to the same artists for years. The consumers who participate in these things do so because they are somehow attached to these celebrities. A person doesn't say his or her favorite actor is Brad Pitt unless they have a history of watching his movies. This history would probably consist of the fan watching several movies starring Brad Pitt, getting to know his acting style, and even memorizing a few quotes from different movies. All of this results in a viewer being attached to this particular actor. So, as an avid fan, if Brad Pitt were to appear on television advertising a certain product, the viewer would most likely consider checking out this item.

Think about it. Why do celebrities want you to know their life stories? Have you ever noticed some of the most popular celebrities have told stories about their childhood at one point? It can be so obvious that it is sometimes overlooked. Do they really care if their fans know about what happened to them at the age of five? I believe this is one of the many ways celebrities and advertisers get fans and buyers to attach to celebrities emotionally. Explaining the hardships and emotions of a certain celebrity can make him or her appear to be a real, more relatable person to consumers. Recording artist Taylor Swift, for example, has a story of success that every stereotypical dorky teenager can relate to. Before the release of her album, *Fearless*, Taylor Swift seemed to be on every talk-show displaying old home videos and reliving the story of her high school years. Audiences were and still are constantly being reminded of how sweet the tall blonde is and how she overcame being bullied in high school. To teenaged girls everywhere, Swift is a role model—a hero, even. They can not only relate to her, some even want to be her: to be able to say what they feel, stand up to bullies and show those bullies there is more to them than their "dorky" appearance. Just like ten-year-old boys want to be able to fly, have x-ray vision, and super strength like Superman. The only difference being, an eighteen-year-old girl will go out and buy Taylor Swift's album, while a ten-year-old boy will beg his mom to buy him a Superman action figure and pajamas for his birthday. In both situations, consumers are convinced by the respective advertisements to go out and purchase the advertised products. So, the fact that Taylor Swift is a good songwriter and a decent singer isn't the only reason why she sold millions of albums.

If you haven't caught on by now, maybe you don't understand exactly what the "Shortcake Strategy" is. The Shortcake Strategy is a marketing tool that is usually used on children. The method got its name from the popular cartoon character Strawberry Shortcake. In the article "Me Against the Media: From the Trenches of a Media Lit Class" by Naomi Rockler-Gladen, she explains in her own words how the Shortcake Strategy began. Tom Engelhardt defines the "'Shortcake Strategy'—[as a concept through] . . . which children's TV shows were created for the exclusive purpose of marketing large collections of children's toys" (Rockler-Gladen 2009:287).

Some do not realize this, but Strawberry Shortcake was not originally a Saturday morning cartoon. Shortcake and her friends were created by American Greetings to sell cards. After the show was created, customers would buy the cards simply because they recognized the characters from the television show. Just as when people of a younger generation notice a Sprite product and the Drake lyrics pop into their head, there are probably millions of people of the 1980s who sing "Straw-ba-ba-ba-ba-berry!" when they notice the little girl's face on a greeting card.

Joy Tashjian and Naidoo Campbell, who wrote "Licensing and Merchandising in Children's Television and Media," which is published in the book *The Children's Television Community*, explain how far this strategy has come. "From toys, clothing, books, video games to toothbrushes, bubble bath, cereal, and snack foods, store shelves are overflowing with products prominently featuring children's television and cartoon characters" (Tashjian and Campbell 2007:165). In 1987, when the concept of advertising to children via popular shows was new, author Cy Schneider released his book titled *Children's Television*. He states, "New children's characters are no longer originated by television or movies. Instead they are originated by toy companies as products, and then turned into television shows" (Schneider 1987:111). Once the producers of a toy realize their product is selling well, they create a show with a plot and new characters to boost the sales even higher. Or vice versa, a popular show can be turned into an even more popular line of toys. Schneider goes on to explain more of the sales strategy, "The theory behind these new shows is that young viewers have already been attracted to the characters in toy form, and will therefore be attracted to the programs. Conversely, the programs help boost retail sales of the existing and new products in these brands categories" (Schneider 1987:112). This is the equivalent to celebrities creating a success story for their audience. The celebrity, not unlike the toy, is seen as popular and admired by fans. Then, similar to a television program, the celebrity comes out with a story from his or her past that people can relate to. Just as the television program helps sell toys, the success story helps boost the sales of albums, movies, or whatever the celebrity is endorsing. So when Kate Hudson discusses her pregnancy with the hosts of *E! News* and then within each commercial break we see her in an Almay commercial endorsing makeup, perhaps viewers should stop and think about why Hudson is doing this. Does she really care if we as viewers know about her future child? Or is it a part of "the program" used to make the audience and buyers like the toy more?

The more the audience likes the celebrity, the more sales this celebrity will produce. Realizing this, companies will hire actresses such as Kate Hudson or hip-hop artists as popular as Drake to make what some may call an endorsement deal. Not only do the celebrities know that connecting to their audience will get them to buy their products, but big companies similar to Nike know this as well. They know that an athlete like David Beckham, who is respected and well known, can help them heighten sales. In the article "Risks and Rewards of Celebrity Endorsements," Anita Elberse (2009) explains how much a celebrity can affect a company's sales: "[S]ales for brands in a variety of consumer-product categories jumped an average of 4 percent in the six months following the start of an endorsement deal . . . Several brands saw sales rise with more than 20 percent . . ."

Now back to Taylor Swift. Since there is not a person in the world who does not like Swift, she can use her talent to not only advertise and sell her own work, but also help other companies be recognized as well. Along with her fellow celebrities, Swift has been in several commercials over the past few years. She has been seen endorsing several different products from video games, cameras, makeup to big name corporations such as Target. Companies like Target realize that someone as personable as Taylor Swift will catch the attention of viewers using her charisma and charm to win them over and convince them to shop at their local Target. The recent Covergirl "Natureluxe" commercials show Swift encouraging viewers to buy Covergirl's new products. With a perfect made-up face, she explains the product as she gracefully frolics through sheer linens. Although it should be clear to the viewer that her words are very scripted and that wearing the new makeup will most likely not make them look anything like Swift, nor will it result in their doing pirouettes through sheer fabric, viewers still buy into it. The same people who like Taylor enough to buy her album are probably in the check-out line at their favorite Target (because Target has made consumers believe Taylor Swift shops there), buying the new "Natureluxe" makeup. It is the same case with the other Cover Girls, Queen Latifah, Drew Barrymore, and Rihanna all relating to a different audience and all persuading them, in a typical scripted commercial way to be "Easy, Breezy, Beautiful."

Consumers should not overlook the fact that celebrities, advertisers, and companies are working together to draw them in by influencing their emotions. Some may feel they cannot be affected by these sale methods, and that they are only used on children, when the reality is that advertisers can find a way to relate to anyone that is willing to listen. Like children, we will create memories with different celebrities through their music, movies, and other works resulting in an emotional response while they are trying to convince us to buy something. There is a reason why they are our favorite celebrities, and as fans we are willing to support them.

Works Cited

Elberse, Anita. "Risks and Rewards of Celebrity Endorsements." *CNN*. 16 Dec. 2009. Web. Apr. 2011. <http://articles.cnn.com/200916/opinion/elberse.athlete.endorsements.tiger.woods_1_endorsers-celebrity-brands?_s=PM:OPINION>.

Rockler-Gladen, Naomi. "Me Against the Media: From the Trenches of a Media Lit Class." Graff, Gerald, Cathy Birkenstein, and Russel K. Durst. *"They Say/I Say": The Moves That Matter in Academic Writing: with Readings*. New York: Norton, 2009. Print.

Schneider, Cy. "The Licensed Character—Today's Hottest Salesman." *Children's Television: the Art, the Business, and How It Works*. Lincolnwood, IL: NTC Business, 1987. Print.

Tashjian, Joy and Campbell, Naidoo. "Licensing and Merchandising in Children's Television and Media." Bryant, J. Alison. *The Children's Television Community*. Mahwah, NJ: Lawrence Erlbaum, 2007. Print. 165–188.

Sarenna Gomes

Without "Nerds," Where Would We Be?

2011 Award for Excellence in Persuasive Writing

In this essay, the writer focuses on a specific contemporary negative stereotype and through a series of examples deconstructs the assumptions that form the crux of the stereotype. Why does the writer place quotation marks around the word nerd? Is there one example of a "nerd" in the essay that is especially striking for you? Do you think that the essay would have been more persuasive if the writer had evoked only real people as examples? In other words, what was the writer's purpose in bringing up fictional "nerds"? In your opinion, could negative stereotypes be "re-conditioned" into positive ideas? Why or why not? As you re-read the essay, take notice of its flow and consider the strategies that the writer used to achieve effective transitions. Finally, how effective do you think is the title of the essay? Do you find the use of the pronoun "we" justified in this style of writing? Why or why not?

This essay doesn't contain a Works Cited page, although the writer makes use of sources. Rather, the writer provided sources in the essay in the way they might appear in a non-academic location, such as in a newspaper or a magazine essay. Would you be able to locate the writer's sources, given the information she had provided?

When we think of the term "nerd" we visualize someone with big-rimmed glasses and pants that are too short, wearing a Star Trek shirt, white socks with brown loafers and maybe even suspenders. There is an echo of a snorting laugh in the background, at a joke that only the techno-savvy could understand.

When one visualizes a "nerd" one probably thinks of someone like Steve Urkel from the television show *Family Matters*. However, both men and women can be "nerds." Steve Urkel looks like a male "nerd" because he wears suspenders, pants that are too short, white socks with brown saddle shoes, shirts buttoned to the neck and big rimmed glasses. He snorts like a pig when he laughs. While a female "nerd" has many of these same characteristics, her wardrobe consists of a plaid skirt, a white blouse (buttoned to the neck) and knee socks; her hair is usually full of hair gel. In high school, "nerds" have braces, and their faces are covered with severe acne or freckles. Their body structure is either skinny like a post or obese beyond compare. Those who mock the nerd feel comfortably superior. Is this really fair? No, it is not. There are many people in our history, both fictional and non-fictional, who at one time or another have been placed in this undistinguished category. However, without these "nerds," where would we be?

A "nerd" is assumed to be obsessed with intellectual or academic pursuits, perhaps a member of the high school math and/or chess teams (as both these clubs require a high intellect). "Nerds" have a fascination with science and math; the stereotype is that they are typically good with numbers and experts in designing and conducting science experiments. At any school science or computer clubs, one can usually find the school "nerds" working on some form of extra credit, solving scientific equations or developing a new computer programming project. They can figure out how to make computers do things faster than anyone else and they know how to fix any issue a computer might have. Additional stereotypes depict "nerds" as having no physical strength or athletic ability. An "intellectual nerd" is assumed to be a sci-fi aficionado who watches *Star Wars* and *The Lord of the Rings*. They also play videogames which deal with magic and wizards and/or read comic books.

The label of "nerd" brings the possibility of perpetual humiliation and even bullying. From junior high through high school, "jocks" and other people who are uncomfortable with the school "nerds" like to mess with a "nerd's" self-esteem. "Nerds" are sometimes shoved into lockers and left there for long periods of time, until someone notices they are missing. They are also pushed into the bathroom by the jocks and given "swirlies" in the toilets. For some, high school is the worst experience of their lives. No "nerd" wants to think about the negative impact of their place in the high school hierarchy because they don't enjoy being beaten up.

In addition, people see "nerds" as immature, weird, and strange. Yet oftentimes it's this group of people who challenge the normal way of doing things; they are nonconformists. They focus on their academic successes and do not get involved with the typical school activities because they are preparing for a better future, not only for themselves but in many cases for society as well.

Bill Gates, founder of Microsoft, is an excellent example of famous "nerd" who proves this point. He was a computer and science "nerd" as a young child. He even wore the big glasses that fit the stereotype of a "nerd." According to the website Biography.com, Bill Gates' interest in computer software programming began at the age of 13. Though accepted to Harvard University, he dropped out after only one year to found Microsoft with Paul Allen. He revolutionized the way we look at and use computers for everything from writing papers, to making presentations, to surfing the Internet. Picture the life of the average college student today if computer technology had not changed in the past 35 years. Today, Bill Gates is one of the richest men in the 21st century.

One might ask, "Where does the negative view of nerds come from?" This social group of people has been around for some time. Oftentimes it's the school bully, insecure teenager or even adults who see themselves as unsuccessful in their own lives that perpetuate cruelty toward the "nerd" stereotype. One has to wonder how much of nerd taunting is due to jealousy of the nerds' creative minds and level of intellect. It seems unfair to treat people in such a manner based on the fact that they are different from the norm.

The nerd stereotype is harmful and demeaning to people who meet the criteria. However, these same people have been some of the most influential in the history of the world. There is another side to nerds that we need to remember. Even the entertainment industry has taken on the stereotypical "nerd" and turned the outcast into the loveable character that we can't live without. There are both non-fictional and fictional people who have proven these stereotypes beside the point.

In addition to Bill Gates, there are many more real-life people who were considered "nerds" in their youth and have gone on to become influential people. Two of these include Albert Einstein and Steve Jobs. Their individual contributions in the areas of science and technology are considered by some to be of the utmost importance to today's society.

Albert Einstein is probably one of the most famous "nerds" in history. Just look at his crazy hair and mustache! He was a theoretical scientist who greatly influenced the field of physics with his discovery of the law of the photoelectric effect, as well as the general theory of relativity. For his contributions to the world of science he won the Nobel Peace Prize for science in 1921. In today's society Einstein would be considered a "nerd" because of his avid interest in math and science. Imagine what the world would be like if he hadn't been a science "nerd."

Steve Jobs, the co-founder of Apple, is yet another example of a famous "nerd." Notable Biographies.com says that when he was young, he showed a great interest in electronics and gadgets, as well as in figuring out how they worked. He was a loner who wasn't interested in team sports or other group activities. All of these are stereotypical attributes of a "nerd." Today Apple is best known for the creation of the Macintosh computer (or "Mac")—a streamlined personal computer. Apple has developed and released the iPod, the iPhone, and the iPad: all considered necessities by today's student. Steve Jobs still fits the stereotype of a "nerd" because he loves working with computers and he has the physical characteristics of a "nerd": tall, lanky, with glasses. However, his dedication to hard work, attention to detail, and his vision of the future of technology has proven that he is a "nerd" to be reckoned with.

Television and movies have portrayed many different types of "nerds." These role models may start out as oddballs or annoying characters, but then find a place in our hearts so that we root for their success. Three examples of these fictional "nerds" include Steve Urkel from the television show *Family Matters*, Velma Dinkley from the cartoon *Scooby-Doo*, and Timothy McGee from the television show *NCIS*. These characters demonstrate that the entertainment world thinks the average "nerd" is a critical part of our society.

For Steve Urkel, science is his life; he creates inventions such as a time machine and the "transformation chamber" that changes Steve to Stephan Urquelle. Steve doesn't seem to care that people see him as odd or as a "nerd"; instead he embraces his oddness and celebrates it. The audience is first annoyed with Steve and all his odd behavior, but then we see that his intentions are pure and he becomes less like a "nerd" whom we want to leave us alone and more like a good friend we are rooting for to succeed.

Velma Dinkley from the *Scooby-Doo* cartoon series is the brains behind the Mystery Inc. Detective Agency. She has thick glasses, and she seems to know something about everything–she's the "nerd" of the group. However, it's Velma to whom the gang looks to figure out the inconsistencies in the mystery they are trying to solve. Her character shows that brains, and not necessarily beauty, are important to reaching one's goals.

Meanwhile, Timothy McGee from the television show *NCIS,* although a "nerd," is the go-to person when his NCIS team needs information about a suspect or a victim from various sources such as phones, computers, and financial or government databases. He is able to find information valuable to solving a case in minutes or hours, rather than days or weeks. Tim is an avid computer gamer with a passion for tactical warfare games. These are all signs of the stereotypical "nerd," yet his team sees past all that "nerdiness" and accepts him as a valued member of their NCIS family. This acceptance—and that of Steve Urkel and Velma Dinkley–shows that a "nerd" is someone we can rely on to get the job done and whom we can respect and love.

Though a "nerd" is typically seen as a negative stereotype, maybe it's time to see it as a positive. "Nerds," both real and fictional, have influenced and changed our lives. They have taught us acceptance and given us computer technology, advances in mathematics and science and so much more. They have changed the way we think and have made major contributions to our society. Without their standing out above the rest, we would be living in the dark ages of typewriters and correction tape, rather than laptops and spell-check. Nerds created and streamlined computers, which once would fill an entire room, but now can fit in the palm of your hand. Without the contributions of "nerds," information would sometimes be impossible to get rather than available at the push of a button. Without "nerds," Neil Armstrong would never have walked on the moon; there would be no vaccine for many childhood diseases like measles, mumps or polio; cancer research would not be as advanced as it has become. In addition, research into alternative forms or energy, alternative sources for fuel, recycling processes and uses for recycled materials would be non-existent. "Nerds" have the ability to change the world. They should be revered, praised and thanked, rather than mocked and ridiculed.

Caitlin Angelo

The Forgotten Holocaust

2010 Award for Excellence in Persuasive Writing

The writer of this essay makes use of a number of print sources, both articles and books, to provide supporting information for her claims. What effect does the use of these sources have on you as a reader? Notice how she weaves her own claims about events and the summaries and paraphrases of her sources. Why does she choose to quote the definition of genocide and Henry Morganthau's observation about the Euphrates River, instead of paraphrasing these items too? The writer chooses to rebut opponents to her claims who cite a lack of documentation of the genocide; is her argument about the amount of first-hand information convincing? Why does this writer end with a paragraph about Armenia's current problems, and the fact that it still maintains a blockade of Turkish goods which largely hurts Armenia? Given what the writer has said, is Armenia's maintenance of the blockade understandable?

In the 1940's, war-torn Europe brought to light the darkest side of the human soul as Nazi soldiers exterminated millions of Jews, gypsies, and other minorities in front of the eyes of the Allied forces. No one could argue that among the many names for this atrocity, the most applicable was "genocide," the systematic and carefully planned extinction of a race of human beings. Just thirty years before, another ethnic cleansing had occurred: that of the Armenians at the hands of the nationalist group the Young Turks. How is it that the educated world is so aware of the Jewish Holocaust and its devastating effects, yet many live in ignorance of the event that in certain ways paved the road for future genocides? The fact remains that as many as two million Armenians were drowned, burned alive, and sold and bartered to brutal masters, resulting in the loss of thousands of years' worth of culture and history (Dadrian 90). Yet this tragedy goes both unpunished and unrecognized; the entire world has moved on past this injustice, allowing the Turks to effectively get away with mass murder. Scholars debate whether or not the event even constitutes "genocide." This lack of punishment or recognition of guilt allowed the Holocaust, as well as more recent genocides in Bosnia, Rwanda, and Sudan, to occur (Melson 91). Extensive first-hand documentation of widespread methods of death and torture of Armenians demonstrates that a group of Turks indeed committed the irreparable act of genocide. Turkey must be held accountable for its actions, and the on-going plight of the Armenians must not be forgotten, in order to help prevent genocides to come.

The relationship between the Ottoman Empire and Armenia had always been tense. The Armenians had a positive relationship with Russia, Turkey's despised enemy. They followed Christianity while the Turks followed Islam. For the Turks, the Armenians were despised minorities that were quite successful and involved in the modern world, rivaling Turkey itself. Even before World War One started, Turkey had committed two smaller mass murders in two separate periods: 80,000–100,000 Armenians from 1894–1896, and 20,000 in 1909 (Bloxham 29). The Young Turks were a group of nationalists in the Ottoman Empire that brought these prejudices and old hatreds to new highs by causing the first genocide of the 20th century.

For a mass murder to be called genocide, it must meet the terms of the official definition of the United Nations. According to Leo Kuper, author of *The Turkish Genocide of Armenians*, there must be intent to destroy all or part of a race of people, brought about by killing members of the group, causing serious bodily harm or mental harm to members of the group, or deliberately inflicting on the group conditions of life calculated to bring about its physical destruction in whole or in part (44).

All of these conditions, and many others, were forced upon the Armenians in carefully calculated ways. The beginning of the end for the Armenians started with deportations. Turkish soldiers forced Armenians to make long and difficult journeys into the deserts of the modern day Syria. Heat, exhaustion, and disease were the primary causes of death; the soldiers furthered these fatalities by brutalizing and starving their victims. The issue of how to deal with the elderly and the children quickly came up, since the Turks were not inclined to kill them personally. They instead released thousands of convicts, giving them explicit freedom to kill and torture without repercussions (Akçam 135). These felons committed the worst of the atrocities: they tied children to planks and set them afire, buried other children alive in mass graves, put babies in "steam baths" to die, and drowned girls they had no interest in keeping alive (Dadrian 423). United States Ambassador Henry Morganthau observed that the number of dead bodies left in the Euphrates River "created such a barrage that the Euphrates changed its course for about a hundred yards" (426). The people who were fortunate enough to survive suffered an even worse fate: the prettiest and youngest girls were sent to the commanding officers or officials as sex slaves or forced into brothels. Soldiers passed through these brothels, bringing diseases and destruction with them. For example, Hu¨seyin Bey, the mayor of a town called Ras-ul-Ain, bragged about raping as many as 60 young Armenian girls with the help of his two sons (427). Women were not alone in these horrors; young boys were often adopted by Turkish families for the sole purpose of being sexually and physically tortured (428). An estimated 1.5 million Armenians were put to death, yet for many, the emotional devastation and brutalization continued. These circumstances are consistent with the conditions of the United Nations' terms for genocide, because 1.5 million Armenians were put to death based on their ethnic classification; many were forced to embark on death marches with the knowledge that most would die (Akçam 147), and both the emotional and physical devastation of the Armenians remained long after the genocide had ended.

How did the world react to the news of this brutality? Within the legal realm, the term "crimes against humanity" was used for the first time during the trials against the perpetrators. (Segesser 107). Humanitarian aid and public interest were strong at first, until the world was swept up in the more pressing dangers of World War One. The first key trial took place in Yozgat, where only two men were found guilty (Lewy 2). By the time of the next major trial, in Istanbul, seven of the key figures involved had fled the country and were tried in absentia and condemned to death, a punishment that was never served, at least by the court officials (4). The British were forerunners in trying to bring justice to the Armenian victims, but even they soon gave in and their representatives stated, "The Armenian claims are not a vital question for the Allies . . . [the British] will not sever their relations with Turkey for the sake of the Armenian question" (Akçam 365), officially stating that the problems of the Armenians were less important than maintaining prosperous relations with Turkey. To this day, Turkey has not even admitted that the events that transpired constituted genocide. Their entrance into the European Union should have been barred because of their continuous denial, yet they were allowed to become a contributing member of the Union, even going so far as to withdraw in dudgeon from several meetings because another nation used the term "genocide" in regards to Armenia ("Denial"). Their continuous denial is an affront to international relations, and an even greater affront to the prevention of future genocides. Adolf Hitler himself inquired of his soldiers in the midst of his plans for the Holocaust, "Who after all is today speaking of the destruction of the Armenians?" (Dadrian 421).

The major argument as to why this butchery does not deserve the term "genocide" is because of faulty documentation. One of the primary sources depicting these events, *The Memoirs of Naim Bey* written by Aram Andonian, has been proven to be a fraud, and most of the court proceedings that took place have been lost (Lewy 11). However a substantial amount of reliable documentation remains to support the claims of genocide. Vahakn N. Dadrian remains one of the leading experts on genocide and has used accounts from the mouths of survivors to publish extensive research on the matter ("Dadrian"). Arnold Joseph Toynbee, a witness to the Armenian slaughter and a member of the British Armenia Committee, released several pamphlets and books, stating the Armenian culture was not nomadic and primitive, but instead civilized and progressive, one easily comparable to Western society (Segesser 100). Franz Werfel lived through the genocide and published numerous plays and novels about it; his novel *The Forty Days of Musa Dagh* is eerily prophetic of future genocides ("Werfel"). Several foreign ambassadors also wrote first-hand accounts of the massacre: Gunduz Aktan of Turkey and Henry Morgenthau of the United States are among the most notable examples (Dekmejian 87). Documentation is quite easily lost over time, but the existing accounts are more than reliable enough to support claims of genocide.

No country wants to admit that they have committed genocide. The Americans, for example, still look back in shame on the murders and forced exile of the Native Americans in US history. Shame is not remorse. A common excuse for Armenian deaths advanced by the Turks is that the Armenian casualties in the early 20th century were simply a byproduct of war. It is true that the Armenians attempted to gather weapons and rally defensive forces after the previous massacres that took place in the late 1890's (Segesser 97). The fact that they did not want to lose another 100,000 people and tried to protect themselves accordingly does not constitute an act of war, especially since their weaponry and defense tactics did little to prevent the greater casualties that began in 1915 (Goudsouzian). Replacing "genocide" with "war" does not make the victims any less helpless or the perpetrators any less guilty. Who among the Turks were drowned, tortured, raped, enslaved, or burned or buried alive? Which Turks were forced to abandon their homes and land; when did the Turks cry out to other nations for help only to be ignored, and which parts of their culture did the Turks lose forever? By excusing what their forefathers did to the Armenians, by labeling it a less unforgiveable title, and as the current appeasement of Turkey indicates, Turkey has effectively gotten away with genocide, for what other name can it be called?

Although the genocide itself occurred almost a century ago, Armenia has never recovered. It is suffering economically; the blockade the Armenians set up against Turkey has had harmful effects on trade and commerce (Goudsouzian). Discussions about removing the blockade have arisen, as it would certainly benefit Armenia financially. But the thought of seeking help from the very country that caused its current financial predicament does not sit well with the Armenian civilians. Economic motives aside, is it time to compromise and forgive? An optimist may say so, yet there is no place for optimism in a country that still vividly remembers its sufferings, the continuous denial of the Turkish government, the lack of punishment of the guilty, and the world that turned its back.

Works Cited

Akçam, Taner. *A Shameful Act: The Armenian Genocide and the Question of Turkish Responsibility.* New York, New York: Henry Holt and Company, LLC., 2006. Print.

Bloxham, Donald. "The Roots of American genocide denial: Near Eastern Geopolitics and the Interwar Armenian Question." *Journal of Genocide Research.* 8.1 (2006): 27–49. Print.

Dadrian, Vahakn N. "Children as victims of genocide: the Armenian case." *Journal of Genocide Research.* 5.3 (2003): 421–438. Print.

Dadrian, Vahakn N. "The Comparative Aspects of the Armenian and Jewish Cases of Genocide: A Sociohistorical Perspective." *Is the Holocaust Unique?* Ed. Alan S. Rosenbaum. Boulder, CO: Westview Press, Inc., 1996. 87–97. Print.

Gale, Thomson. "Dadrian, Vahakn N." *Contemporary Authors Online.* n.p., 26 April 2007. 29 October 2009.

Gale, Thomson. "Franz Werfel." *Contemporary Authors Online.* n.p., 2 October 2003. 29 October 2009.

Goudsouzian, Tanya. "Armenians Angry Over Turkey Accords." *Al Jazeera (Qatar)* 24 October 2009. Print.

Kuper, Leo. "The Turkish Genocide of Armenians, 1915–1917." *The Armenian Genocide in Perspective.* Ed. Richard G. Hovannisian. New Brunswick, New Jersey: Transaction, Inc., 1986. 43–59. Print.

Lewy, Guenter. "Revisiting the Armenian Genocide." *Middle East Quarterly*. 12.4 (2005): 3–12. Print.

Melson, Robert F. "The Armenian Genocide as Precursor and Prototype of Twentieth-Century Genocide."*Is the Holocaust Unique?* Ed. Alan S. Rosenbaum. Boulder, CO: Westview Press, Inc., 1996.87-97. Print.

Segesser, Daniel Marc. "Dissolve or Punish? The International Debate Amongst Jurists and Publicists on the Consequences of the Armenian Genocide for the Ottoman Empire, 1915–23." *Journal of Genocide Research*. 10.1 (2008): 95–110. Print.

"Turkey, Armenia, and Denial." Editorial. *The New York Times*. ed. 16 May 2006: A1. Print.

James McMorrow Jr.

A Twisted World

2009 Award for Excellence in Persuasive Writing

Sometimes humor can be a persuasive tool. In this essay, the author engages in a technique called reductio ad absurdum *(persuading by taking a concept to an absurd conclusion) by imagining a world where political decisions are made by popular celebrities, instead of by our current elected officials. If done poorly, this technique can seem mean-spirited, but by using the words* we *and* our *in the last paragraph, the writer identifies himself with the Americans he is mildly critiquing. As you read this essay, consider your own reactions to the author's arguments.*

As America is led down the seemingly inevitable road of doom, courtesy of our fine leaders like Rod Blagojevich, I am left to wonder what the country would look like if we replaced politicians with the people we cared most about, celebrities.

This country would obviously look and run very differently. First off, our capitol would be moved to Hollywood, California, and Washington D.C. would be replaced by a real mall. Janice Dickinson and Joan Rivers would have their most recent faces carved into Mount Rushmore, a place where they (their faces) will never age again. Presidential debates would occur in front of the American Idol judges. I can just picture Simon Cowell telling a candidate how pathetic his healthcare plan is. The 12th Amendment would be changed, eliminating the Electoral College. Instead the president would be chosen by the popular vote; voters would be able to call or text their choice in as many times as they want between 10 pm and midnight.

Shortly after these celebrities are in office, there would be a giant push for the legalization of marijuana and most other drugs. DUIs would be reduced to a simple citation. Marriage laws would be changed and obtaining a divorce would be as easy as ordering a Happy Meal. Respectable newspapers such as The *Wall Street Journal* and *USA Today* would be replaced with *The National Enquirer* and *People*; CNN and CSPAN would be replaced by E!, MTV, and VH1; *The Hills* would be considered a documentary. The Supreme Court would be settling big cases such as *Aniston vs. Jolie* and *Cyrus vs. Gomez*. Plastic surgery would replace baseball and become the national pastime. And Oscar, Emmy, and Grammy nights would be national holidays.

There would be a lot of new foreign policies too. The effort to rebuild Iraq would be completely abandoned and replaced with movements to bring feminism, culture, and fashion to the Middle East. Africa would benefit, seeing a significant increase in the effort to battle

HIV and AIDS so that eventually these diseases would be brought under control. Our military would be given a fresh, bold, new look; traditional uniforms would be replaced with color coordinated attire from the top fashion designers. Our troops would be driving Escalades rather than Humvees. The sight of a tricked out Caddy with machine guns, blaring Kanye West, would be enough to send any terrorist running. The terror threat levels would be changed to something all celebrities can relate to: (from lowest to highest) designer, last year's style, knock off, discount, and generic brand.

As if things could not get any better, many changes would be made to our Constitution. The issue of separation of church and state would finally be resolved when the first amendment is changed to eliminate freedom of religion and convert us all to Scientology. An amendment would be added to the Constitution repealing the third amendment, only instead of housing soldiers, it would be mandatory for citizens, depending on wealth, to house and adopt at least two children from foreign countries. A 30th Amendment would be added to legalize gay marriage in all 50 states, while Amendment 31 would repeal the 12th, to change the way the vice president is elected. Instead of candidates running together on a ballot or even having two separate elections, the vice president would be chosen on the TV show, *Bret Michael's: Rock of Gov.*

While I would love to see the day when we have Tom Cruise as president, Oprah as vice president, and a cabinet consisting of Secretary of Defense Arnold Schwarzenegger, Secretary of the Interior Martha Stewart, Secretary of Commerce Donald Trump, and Attorney General 50 Cent, I realize it is very far fetched. Looking at what the nation would look like if celebrities ran it, it should be clear that the people we have put in office are the ones best suited there. As citizens we are a bit too quick to judge how our political representatives have done their jobs. We need to realize that in order to dig ourselves out of this massive hole we are in, it is up to us to be patient, no matter how difficult that may be in times of hardship. Clearly, things could be worse.

Researched Writing

Emma Jones

Evaluation of *Silent Spring*

2013 Award for Excellence in Researched Writing

*In this essay, the primary evidence used by the writer to make her argument is research from external sources. As you examine the paper and its structure, take note of how the writer deftly weaves quotations into the narrative, uses specific direct quotes to highlight salient points, and paraphrases material where necessary. Further, if you examine the end matter, you will notice a Works Cited page **and** a Working Bibliography. Consider why there might be two lists of sources. What needed to be cited in the body and in a Works Cited page? And what sources merely informed the work?*

Finally, as you read, notice the types of sources used. Some are web sources, others are print material. Some of the web sources are not from academic databases. Does this make a difference in how you view the research? Do any of these sources work better for a researched writing essay? Which sources hold more credibility than others? Why?

"'Miss Carson, what do you eat?' 'Chlorinated hydrocarbons like everyone else.'" ("Rachel Carson: 1907–1964")

Rachel Carson's *Silent Spring*, published in 1962, altered the course of history and changed people's attitude toward nature for generations to come. It is rare for a book to shift the entire world's perspective on such a topic. Carson did just this by challenging the judgment of the industries distributing chemicals (i.e., pesticides), but by also challenging the general public to take part in questioning the short and long term effects of using chemicals like DDT. *Silent Spring*, a nonfiction work focusing on Environmental Science, is credited for being the final shove needed to initiate the environmental movement, and for also taming the "control of nature" mentality of people. Reading *Silent Spring* is an essential part of understanding the interrelationship between nature and people's actions, and also what actions people can take to ensure that the footprints left behind are not destructive. *Silent Spring* is a work that many generations should treasure, so that humanity can begin creating a sustainable, secure future.

Rachel Carson was born in Springdale, Pennsylvania, and her love of nature as well as in writing erupted at a very young age. Carson was encouraged by her mother to embrace nature and indulge in its wonders. After graduating from Parnassas High School, she went on to attend the Pennsylvania College for Women to pursue an undergraduate degree in English, but soon after switched to Biology. She then attended graduate school at The Johns Hopkins University where she then earned a Master's degree in Zoology as well as Genetics in 1932. Carson developed a strong interest in sea life, which then led her to further postgraduate research at the Woods Hole Marine Biological Laboratory in Massachusetts. Carson was teaching, but, after the sudden death of her father in 1936, decided that she needed to find regular work and was hired by the U.S. Bureau of Fisheries (the U.S. Fish and Wildlife Service) in Washington, D.C.

Her fascination with marine life led to her first book, *Under the Sea Wind* (1941). Carson later published *The Sea Around Us* (1951), which proved to be a better success than her previous book. What made *The Sea Around Us* different than *Under the Sea Wind* was that it allowed nonscientists, or "laymen," to understand the sea's history and biological importance. This same approachable style was seen again in Carson's *Silent Spring*.

While working on *Silent Spring,* Carson faced many challenges, such as the death of her mother and being diagnosed with cancer. Carson persevered and finished *Silent Spring*, ultimately paving the way for the environmental movement. Carson received many awards for her work, including the Gold Medal of the New York Zoological Society and the John Burroughs Medal for Excellence in Natural History Writing. Despite Carson dedicating her life to studying wildlife, biological systems within the environment, and receiving numerous acknowledgments for her dedication, there were still critics who sought to discredit her work.

Some of the criticisms Carson received not only attempted to discredit her work itself, but her as a person. These acts of *Ad Hominem* arguments made against Carson were relentless. Carson was described as a "quiet, private person, fascinated with the workings of nature from a scientific and aesthetic point of view" ("Rachel Carson: 1907–1964"), but this did not keep her critics from claiming that Carson knew nothing about the scientific area of study. Carson's primary attackers were chemical company representatives or industry scientists. Carson, sticking true to her quiet, private self, rarely responded to any personal attacks. She said in an interview that she would "let the book speak for itself" ("Rachel Carson: 1904–1965") to anyone who was willing to read it, of course.

The main reason why Carson received so much criticism was because many believed she was against the complete use of pesticides. William Darby, one of the harshest critics of Carson, chair of the Biochemistry Department at Vanderbilt University, and known for his review of *Silent Spring* around the time it was published, suggested that Carson's book would be "the end of human progress" (qtd. in Smith). Darby, as well as many other scientists and workers who relied on the economic success pesticides brought, believed that if Carson was taken seriously, there would be a complete economic collapse that will only make things worse.

In fact, Carson was not arguing for the elimination of pesticides, but wanted those responsible to stop indiscriminately distributing pesticides without any consideration of ecological consequences. Carson did not discard science's benefits to humanity in using pesticides, but only "shook her finger at the careless, regressive path science had taken with regard to pesticides" (qtd. in Smith 2001). Carson does describe the harmful effects that pesticides could and *did* bring about. However, at no point in *Silent Spring* did Carson directly say that she was *for* the banning of such chemicals. Carson brought to the attention of many oblivious persons the consequences of using pesticides indiscriminately. Regardless, many blame Carson for the banning of some pesticides, primarily DDT, even though Carson died eight years before the Environmental Protection Agency (EPA) issued its decision to ban DDT. *RachelWasWrong .org* issued a statement directly blaming Carson for the devastation that the banning of DDT brought along in regards to control of human disease: "In fact, today millions of people around the world suffer the painful and often deadly effects of malaria because one person sounded a false alarm. That person is Rachel Carson . . . ," (qtd. in Smith 2001). Carson herself was not entirely responsible for causing the government to reconsider its regulations on DDT. However, she is thought to have stirred up enough controversy to get the movement actually going, leading to the banning of DDT. Another thing to point out is that there are many countries that banned DDT, but there are also many countries that are still using DDT to fight diseases like malaria.

Many others helped to make the environmental movement possible, but Carson's approach in *Silent Spring* on the issue of pesticide regulation made her more iconic. Yaakov Garv, a scholar, compared *Silent Spring* to Murray Bookchin's *Our Synthetic Environment,* which was published earlier in 1962. Bookchin identified many of the same concerns Carson did, but the major difference was each author's approach. Carson took more of a risk in confronting and questioning the structure of capitalism. Garv explains that Carson's credibility would have been strengthened if she had addressed the hurting economy and examined why extensive pesticide use was necessary in the first place. It is understandable that many critics may have wanted Carson to do this because it would have made her arguments less biased. Carson did not choose to do this for an obvious reason: She wanted to get her point across, and only hers.

William Darby was also known for issuing sexist remarks against Carson. Darby's review titled "Silence, Miss Carson!" appeared in *Chemical and Engineering News* (1962). The title itself expressed the attitude of many critics of Carson who were mainly men. These men felt that Carson was an uninformed woman who did not know what she was talking about and was speaking in a man's world, the "inner sanctum of masculine science" (qtd. in Smith 2001). Others claimed that Carson was too emotional, irrational, and sentimental in expressing her arguments. Carson was passionate about nature, and that especially showed in *Silent Spring*. It is expected that Carson would be dramatic about an issue that she felt needed to be taken very seriously. Also, adding emotion into *Silent Spring* worked in Carson's favor because this is how she was able to produce a strong connection between herself and her readers, as well as a strong response from readers.

Carson's credibility as not only a scientist but a writer should not be discredited. In making *Silent Spring* very approachable to the general public, Carson uses imagery and real-life anecdotes to propose solutions to the problems as effectively and persuasively as possible. She uses imagery to enable her readers to visualize the beauty in nature that should be preserved, such as in the opening chapter "A Fable for Tomorrow." Carson paints a picturesque image of a glorious town where life is abundant and in a natural state, but suddenly begins to transform into a wasteland: "Then a strange blight crept over the area and everything began to change. Some evil spell had settled on the community: mysterious maladies swept the flocks of chickens; the cattle and sheep sickened and died. Everywhere was a shadow of death" (Carson 2002:2). The words "strange," "evil," "mysterious," and "death" create a devastating scene in the minds of readers. Carson makes it clear at the end of the chapter that this town does not exist, but it may easily happen to many real towns, if it has not already. Carson also uses anecdotes shared by the general public to act as evidential support. In "No Birds Sing," Carson writes about the town of Hinsdale, Illinois, where a housewife wrote to Robert Cushman Murphy, Curator Emeritus of Birds at the American Museum of Natural History: "Here in our village the elm trees have been sprayed for several years. When I moved here six years ago, there was a wealth of bird life. . . . After several years of DDT spray, the town is almost devoid of robins and starlings. . . . " (Carson 2002:103). Many observations noted by the public, such as this housewife's, contributed to Carson's writing *Silent Spring* in hopes that people could change before it was too late.

In addition to all of the criticisms, others felt that the potential solutions Carson proposed would actually add onto the damage of those affected by the bad economy. Carson's solutions were thought to be unrealistic because pesticides were necessary in order to produce crops and get rid of horrid pests. However, the alternatives Carson proposes do seem realistic in regard to all of the scientific advancements humankind has been able to achieve. In "Beyond the Dreams of the Borgias," Carson suggests two reasonable solutions where one is simply educating the general public about which harmful chemicals to avoid when purchasing insecticides, while the other involves an alternative to ridding of pests: "Agricultural use of insect diseases . . . is already being tried in California, and more extended tests of this method are under way. A great many other possibilities exist for effective insect control by methods that will leave no residues on foods" (Carson 2002:184). Like these proposals, Carson's other alternatives, such as pushing for more research into other methods of agriculture, are doable. As for research, Carson states that money being used to produce these chemicals can go to research into seeking better, healthier alternatives.

The contents of *Silent Spring* work well to support her claim in regulating the use of chemicals in the environment. *Silent Spring* fits into the subject of Environmental Science. Carson had the scientific research to make *Silent Spring* a scientific "novel" and the writing skills to make it a good read. In the final few sentences of Darby's review of *Silent Spring,* he recommends that those who would enjoy *Silent Spring* are "the organic gardeners, the anti-fluoride leaguers, the worshippers of 'natural foods', and those who cling to the philosophy of a vital principle, and pseudo-scientists and faddists" (qtd. in Smith 2001). Darby's recommendation of *Silent Spring* fails to credit *Silent Spring* with the integrity it deserves. Although *Silent Spring* is Carson's attempt to inform the general public and educate anyone who would like to understand the effects human actions have on earth and, most importantly, how to sustain a better planet, those pursuing a career in the sciences, particularly the life sciences, should take interest in this book.

Works Cited

Carson, Rachel. *Silent Spring: The Classic That Launched the Environmental Movement.* Boston: Houghton Mifflin, 2002. Print.

"Rachel Carson: 1907–1964." PBS. PBS, n.d. Web. 16 Mar. 2013.

Smith, Michael B. "'Silence, Miss Carson!' Science, Gender, and the Reception of *Silent Spring.*" *Feminist Studies* 27.3 (2001): 733. Academic Search Premier. Web. 20 Mar. 2013.

Working Bibliography

Carson, Rachel. *Silent Spring: The Classic That Launched the Environmental Movement.* Boston: Houghton Mifflin, 2002. Print.

Dasch, Pat. "Rachel Carson." *Water: Science and Issues.* Ed. E. Julius Dasch. New York: Macmillan Reference USA, 2003. Biography In Context. Web. 19 Mar. 2013.

Hecht, David K. "How To Make A Villain: Rachel Carson and the Politics of Anti-Environmentalism." *Endeavour* 36.4 (2012): 149–155. Academic Search Premier. Web. 20 Mar. 2013.

"Rachel Carson: 1907–1964." PBS. PBS, n.d. Web. 16 Mar. 2013.

"Rachel Carson Dies of Cancer." *Environmental Issues: Essential Primary Sources.* Ed. Brenda Wilmoth Lerner and K. Lee Lerner. Detroit: Gale, 2006. 57–60.Biography In Context. Web. 19 Mar. 2013.

"Rachel Carson Dies of Cancer; 'Silent Spring' Author Was 56." *The New York Times*, April 15, 1964.

Smith, Michael B. "'Silence, Miss Carson!' Science, Gender, and the Reception of *Silent Spring.*" *Feminist Studies* 27.3 (2001): 733. Academic Search Premier. Web. 20 Mar. 2013.

Andrea L. Silva

The Downfall of Civilization and How Spell Check Just Corrected Me

2012 Award for Excellence in Researched Writing

In this essay, the writer employs irony to explore a serious topic: the devastating impact of technology on our enjoyment of and connection with literature and reading. The writer takes us on a journey of researching this topic by relying on the exact medium that she seems to blame for the untimely demise of the reading culture: the Internet. This essay is an example of a nontraditional research paper that draws from the creative non-fiction genre to incorporate striking images, metaphors, and irony to express its points. As you read the essay, pay attention to how the writer describes the steps in her research and consider the impact of the revelations that the writer makes about herself. In your opinion, how do you think the author of this essay feels about giving up traditional sources of information for the ease of the Internet and television?

When you are young, there is great excitement in getting a new book: It's like an unpredictable adventure or a movie, but all in your head. Recently, this has been changing, and the age when reading books becomes a pesky chore has been getting younger and younger. At which date in history was the day that literature died? I searched my online calendar and also googled for the answer, but found nothing to end my wondering. However, with a few good old-fashioned readings, I believe I just may have found the approximate date when literature was secretly murdered.

The most common literature printed on paper is the newspaper. Ever since the first newspaper, the *Acta Diurna* in 59 B.C.E., people have been informed about news and events through the printed word ("World" 2011). After using Google to find a link to the sale of newspapers, I found that for the past 23 years newspaper sales have been dropping. After clicking on another Google link, I found that in 2008 newspaper sales fell by six billion copies in only six months ("Newspaper" 2011). The morning routine of reading the newspaper and having a cup of coffee is changing to watching television and having that cup of coffee. But recognizing the last year as the year when literature died just seemed too early in the past, so I continued my investigation.

My next task was to find out when book sales (ones made of actual paper) started declining. Google surprisingly had no answer for me this time and left me feeling almost lost. It is extremely rare that Google doesn't have an answer to a question. So I thought "When did I stop reading books for entertainment?" Well, the answer to that question would have to be when I turned on my television and became a Teenage Mutant Ninja Turtles fanatic: that show was really just a trap to mesmerize children at the devastating age of four or five. The Teenage Mutant Ninja Turtles allowed my mind to reject books for extreme turtle action (and pizza). It now seems likely that television killed literature. Television has probably been the major reason for the newspaper sales decline since TV spreads news with videos, attractive newscasters, and fancy music. I can't even recall the last time I saw a paperboy. Why spend more than 10 seconds reading about one accident when you can see all the blood and gore while barely using your brain? I believe television is standing over literature's grave not allowing it to rise from the dead, but who was the actual murderer?

The only object I use more than a television set is my computer. I finally believed I finished solving the mystery and did so by using the murderer. The computer is the only device that has managed to capture books, newspapers, and moving images to display them with the touch of a fingertip. After seeing a YouTube video about the current status of the war in the Middle East, why would I ever go to the trouble of turning those giant goofy newspaper pages again? Computers make reading an actual book seem like a chore much like raking leaves or doing other housework. They discount the words in favor of pictures and pictures in favor of video (Gelernter 1994:300).

At this point, I came to my mind that I was the one controlling this computer. I then realized the blood of literature reddened my fingertips. What a twisted and crude moment of reality to find out I was the actually murderer of literature. As I thought more and more about the murder, I realized how guilty I really was. It is time to confess my role in the incident. I have used Google ever since my family bought a computer, and I have not been to the library since. Instead of reading books, I go to Sparknotes.com. There is no Shakespeare dialogue in my memory, just a simple description of the plot. I am sure I am not the only person to have not read a single conversation or a detailed depiction since computers have become popular. This can't be good, for intellectual talk will become a thing of the past, and everyone will talk in slang. Instead of buying newspapers, I watch television or just look up the event on Google. The amount of actual reading in my life is shrinking every day. Even while doing this paper, I will admit that I have become so repulsed by large forms of literature that when I cited Newsosaur, paragraph one, I really just read the title of the article.

And yet I will not take full blame for the murder of literature. Every person today is also responsible for its death. We all watch so much television that it has become worthwhile for companies to spend millions of dollars on just one thirty-second advertisement. We think that we become more productive and smarter, but in reality our computers are just becoming part of our brain. People do not think that there is too much television in their lives for as computers are getting smarter, people may be getting dumber.

Works Cited

Gelernter, D. (1994). Unplugged: The Myth of Computers in the Classroom. In G. Muller, *The McGraw-Hill Reader* (10th ed., pp. 299–302). New York: McGraw-Hill.

"World Association of Newspapers—A Newspaper Timeline." *WAN*. N.p., n.d. Web. 1 Nov. 2011. <www.wan-press.org/article2822.html>.

"Newspaper Sales Fall Record 3B in 6 Mos." Newsosaur. Web. Nov 1, 2011. http://newsosaur.blogspot .com/2008/09/newspaper-sales-fall-record-3b-in-6-mos.html

Allison Egger

Love the One You Click

2011 Award for Excellence in Researched Writing

In this essay, the writer analyzes the pros and cons of online dating services. Egger takes on a less popular position and is successful in maintaining it throughout the essay. The writer carefully considers the opposing view and presents a rebuttal, while conceding that individual counter-examples might exist. Notice how the writer uses transitions and alternates between complex and simple sentence structures to achieve a nice rhythm in the piece. As you read the essay, consider what the writer's main argument is. Do you find it convincing? Why or why not? What is the opposing view? Does the writer provide evidence for both positions? What might be the purpose of doing this? In your opinion, how could presenting both sides of the issue strengthen the writer's argument?

The average man is about two inches taller online than he is in real life, and the average woman weighs a few pounds less in digital form, but outside of a few tweaks people make to their online physiques, a person's identity is becoming more and more tied to the digital cloud ("Online Dating Stats Reveal the Lies Men & Women Tell"). Whereas in the past it was necessary to pick up the telephone or send a letter in order to get in touch with someone, communication in today's world is just a few clicks away. Whether it be through email, text message, tweets, or Facebook, in our world of ever-present technology, we are always connected to one another. People are spending less and less time communicating in person, and though people will never cease entirely to communicate in the flesh, the need for direct human to human interaction is undoubtedly less than it was a mere decade ago. Therefore it should be no surprise that the world of dating has moved to the Internet too. Some have argued that online dating is ruining the dating world and damaging human communication skills. However, online dating is just a result of changing norms and has improved the world of dating by opening the doors for everyone to be able to go out and date.

In its infancy, the internet was a Wild West of sorts. Few could accurately foresee its future, yet an entire generation was instantly and indelibly mesmerized by the possibilities this new medium held. At first the Internet resembled a barren wasteland. The few available sites were mostly text, and with slow dial-up connections, necessarily so. Slowly, bandwidth increased and photos began popping up. Audio could be downloaded. Soon, people could stream video and chat in real time. As the Internet expanded in size, its popularity boomed, and as more and more people found themselves connected, this now-adolescent technology began to find its niche. New business models were created, taking advantage of the efficiencies the internet could create. People took to sending emails to far off friends and relatives, giving them an easier, cheaper means of communication. Eventually, social networking was born, and with it people's lives began to move onto the web.

It is important to note that although people are spending increasingly more time online, human beings will always exist first and foremost in the physical world. According to "Americans Spending A Lot of Time On Social Networking Sites" (www.worldclasscommunications. com), Americans are spending close to 60% of their time on their mobile internet devices or social networking sites. While people may spend time 'socializing' on Facebook, and 'talking' via text messages, and human to human interaction may be decreasing, real-life exchanges will always be a necessity. The same is true with online dating. While some people have claimed that spending so much time on the Internet is creating a generation that is incapable of face to face communication, there is no evidence to support such a conclusion, and the fact remains that people today are keeping in touch with and dating more people than ever before.

The days of falling in love with your high school sweetheart and getting married right after graduation are gone. According to the U.S. Census, the median marrying age is currently nearly twenty-six for women and nearly twenty-eight for men, the highest since they started keeping track in 1890 ("Sooner vs. Later"). In addition, people's view on the ideal age for marriage has also changed. According to a Gallop poll taken in 1946, most people thought the ideal age for marriage to be twenty-five for men and twenty-one for women. Gallop took another survey of about five hundred adults in 2008 and found that people's ideal age for marriage had risen to twenty-seven for men and twenty-five for women ("Sooner vs. Later").

One of the main reasons that the marriage age has risen is that more people are concentrating on putting their education and careers first and their love lives second. In the *USA Today* article "Sooner vs. Later: Is There an Ideal Age for 1st Marriage?" sociologist Andrew Cherin of John Hopkins University says, "People are more concerned with their own self development than they used to be. People are postponing marriage until everything in their lives is in working order. The order means after you've finished your education, perhaps after beginning your career, and increasingly after you've lived with your partner. They're postponing marriage until they think they're ready for it." Waiting later in life to marry has proven to be a good idea; people who marry before the age of twenty are two to three times more likely to divorce ("Sooner vs. Later"). Online dating is helping open doors for those who are waiting later in life to find love by giving them a easy and convenient medium to try dating.

Online dating is simply a byproduct of this shift in priorities. If education and profession are taking precedence over love and finding a mate is put on hold until the mid to late twenties, the historically common practice of meeting one's soul-mate in high school or college becomes impossible. If a twenty-six year old is finally secure enough in her job to begin searching for love, it is far less likely that she is living near, or even still in touch with, most of her high school or college friends. She likely lives in a city different than the one in which she grew up or attended college, sees her closest high school and college friends on rare occasions, and socializes mostly with her colleagues, who due to company policy, are off limits. She can go to bars every Saturday, volunteer every Sunday, and participate in an uncomfortable number of social events, but the odds of her finding someone to love are still fewer than if she simply uploaded a few pictures onto an online dating site. The reason people choose to meet over the internet, then, is not due to lack of communication skills. They hold real world jobs, interact daily with real world people, and have many real world friends. There will always be some anti-social, awkward people who do not interact well with other human beings (there always have been), but many of the people using online dating websites can simply hear the ticking of their biological clocks and therefore must expand their dating pool. They will continue to interact, person to person, in their real world spheres of work, friendship, and love, and in that way will never lose the ability to communicate face to face.

One of the advantages of the online dating world, and one of the main reasons people turn to it, is that it is so large and so varied. According to research done by the Internet analysis company Hitwise and published in "Love Actually . . . Virtually" in *The Straight Times* (Singapore) there are now 1,378 different dating sites, up from 876 in 2005. Two of the most popular are Match.com and Eharmony.com. Match.com claims that if you are looking for marriage, you are more likely to find your mate online than at a bar, and online dating is the third most popular mate finding method, behind only meeting through an acquaintance or at work or school ("Marriage-minded Do Better Online"). In the same article, *Online Dating Magazine* estimates that 120,000 Americans who marry each year have met online. This popularity has created a snowball effect. As more people join these sites, it becomes more acceptable to do so, which leads to more people joining the sites. Now, users aren't afraid to admit to others that they have tried dating online. Joe Tracy, publisher of *Online Dating Magazine,* says that "Online dating is by now a preferred way for singles to find dates. I think that the stigma that has been attached to online dating, and there's still some of that today, has greatly decreased. Everybody knows someone who has done online dating so people find and pursue potential mates." Someone who might never have considered dating before would most likely feel more comfortable trying it if their good friend had tried it before and had told them about their experience.

Along with millions of users, online dating offers specialty sites that offer the convenience of being able to narrow the playing field of possible suitors by finding something in common with each other. For example, a Jewish person only interested in another fellow Jew might want to try Jdate.com, a vegetarian looking to share a salad could try greenfriends.com, while a gold digger might just want to peruse sugardaddy.com. These so called "niche sites" are helping to pair people by their preferences, whether it be interests, ethnicity, religion, or even physical appearance. Getting people together that have similarities not only helps finding a match easier and quicker, but also helps to eliminate those all too frequent awkward first dates where one person has nothing in common with the other, leading to awkward conversation and even more awkward silence.

And while online dating allows picking a potential mate based on extremely narrow, user entered criteria, it is also capable of opening up the field of potential mates. If a user wants a 28 year old male between 5'11" and 6'1" who weighs between 175 and 195 pounds, likes reading, skiing, cats and *Greys Anatomy*, she can find him. But if a user simply wants to begin conversation with as many potential suitors as possible, she can do that too. It is in this way that online dating is able to be so effective. In just minutes it is possible to peruse more mates online than one could meet in over a month of bar-hopping.

Some have argued that online dating, along with other social networking sites, are bad for society. In the article "Rise of Sofalising is the New Social Trend" published on Walesonline .co.uk, author Adel Blake argues that society today is a victim of "sofalising," or people being more comfortable communicating with their friends through electronic communication rather than actually going out and interacting with people. In the article Blake interviews Dr. David Lewis, a cognitive neurophysiologist, who says that the danger in "sofalising" is that without going out and interacting with people "you can appear to have a very good social life without having to invest much time or effort in it." In "Where the Computer is God and the Internet the Umbilical Cord," author Sumit Raina warns that "We have lost the human touch. We were born to live in a society, not in some virtual world where people fake their identities. After all, we are not robots. We have feelings and emotions which a programmed computer can never understand." While these points may hold some validity, and it may be true that people are communicating more through electronic means, this point of view fails to see the bigger picture. Although there may be some people who spend almost all of their free time on the internet, most simply use it as a springboard to more personal interaction. The electronic communication is usually only the ice breaker that often leads to a face to face conversations and the possibility of more.

The problems that so many people seem to have with these sites are that all interaction takes place in the virtual world, that these people don't actually converse, and that what you see online is not necessarily what you get in person. While these are all valid arguments, they simply do not apply to the reality of what online dating services represent. Sites like Eharmony and Match.com are simply platforms for introduction. As Facebook is a network of virtual communities, online dating sites are practically virtual bars. In the physical world a person might go to a bar, strike up a conversation with a dashing young lady, buy her a drink and ask for her number; in the virtual world he would do much the same thing. He would go to Match.com, strike up a written correspondence with a dashing young lady, send her an e-wink, and ask her on a date. In both cases the real wooing begins after the initial introduction. Online dating sites are really not online *dating* sites. They are more like online *meeting* sites. And while this may seem like a slight distinction, it makes a huge difference when looking at their long-term societal effects.

What we need to understand is that these websites are merely filling a need created by an already momentous shift in how modern society conducts itself. With more single, young adults than ever before, it has become a necessity to create new forums for introduction, and with these young adults already spending so much time online, the Internet becomes this forum. All these dating sites have done is move the meat market that is the single bar scene to the Internet, and in so doing they have civilized the process of introduction. Whereas a typical initial conversation at a bar consists of drunken, cheesy pick-up lines and drunken, bad decisions, an initial conversation online is more of an actual dialogue, with each side of the potential couple asking serious questions and giving thought to serious answers. Decisions can be made rationally, based on compatibility, and over a period of time when the relationship begins online. In a bar, all that is considered are base desires, impulse, and initial attractiveness, which although good, important things, will lend themselves more towards short, bad relationships than long, meaningful ones.

Regardless of where a couple meets, however, the courting process remains grounded in the real world. No amount of email communication can replace time spent with a potential suitor, and no has said it should. Instead, these dating sites allow people to move seamlessly from the virtual world to the physical. Dating sites are also proving to lead to intimacy within the relationship faster. According to a survey performed by Online Schools, one in three U.S. women who meet a man online have sex on the date with the man. The survey also found that the average courtship time decreased when meeting someone online to 18.5 months, as compared to the 42 month courtship of people who met offline ("Online Dating Stats Reveal the Lies Men & Women Tell"). This is most likely the result of the advantage online daters have. By taking the time to get to know each other, learning what commonalities they share, and gaining a sense of comfort before actually having to meet in person, an online couple that chooses to pursue a relationship has a solid foundation upon which to quickly build.

Despite the growing popularity and numbers of users of online dating sites, people still have their fears. The anonymity of the computer makes it easy for liars and predators to blend with the good, honest users. Jennifer Perry, a spokesperson for e-victims.org was quoted in the article "Avoiding Mr. Wrong on the Net" as saying, "There's something about the net that can make women who are normally cautious drop their guard." But how is being lied to online (and potentially being hurt) any more dangerous than picking up a random person at a bar? There are predators in the real world, too, and while it is possible to tell what someone looks like in real life, it can be just as hard to identify a predator in person as it is online. It is not the technology that makes dating dangerous, it is the people.

In spite of these fears, online dating continues to grow in both popularity and acceptance. As people continue to delay marriage, and a generation grows up having never known the stigma attached to having an online dating profile, these sites will continue to prosper. As technology continues to improve and video chat becomes more commonplace, people will be able to talk face to face to potential suitors, making it easier still to know a great deal about a person before meeting in person. There will always be a segment, and possibly even a majority, of the population that begins relationships solely in the physical world, but the number of relationships started online will surely continue to rise.

All great advances in civilization have been a product of technology. Fire, the wheel, the printing press and the telephone all created a shift in how society functioned. We are in the midst of the next revolution: the internet is changing the world once again, making society more efficient than it ever was before. But no matter what new technology comes along, human to human interaction remains paramount to society. Internet dating cannot change that. Although some will argue that technology is diminishing the personal aspect of relationships, online dating will continue to balance the efficiencies of the Internet with the warmth of real, physical intimacy.

Works Cited

"Americans Spending a Lot of Time on Social Networking Sites." *www.worldclasscommunications.com*. World Class Communications, n.d. Web. 10 Dec. 2010.

Blake, Aled. "Rise of Sofalising is the New Social Trend." *www.walesonline.co.uk*. Ed. Aled Blake. N.p., 18 Nov. 2010. Web. 6 Dec. 2010.

Gwee, Stephanie. "Love Actually, Virtually." *The Straits Times* 29 July 2008. *Lexis Nexis Academic*. Web. 6 Dec. 2010.

Jayson, Sharon. "Sooner vs. Later: Is There an Ideal Age for First Marriage?" *www.usatoday.com*. N.p., 9 Nov. 2008. Web. 6 Dec. 2010.

Jones, Caroline. "Avoiding Mr. Wrong on the Net." *The Mirror* 15 Jan. 2010. *Lexis Nexis Academic*. Web. 6 Dec. 2010.

"Online Dating Stats Reveal The Lies Men & Women Tell." *www.datingsecretsformen.com*. Online Schools, n.d. Web. 10 Dec. 2010.

Raina, Sumit. "Where the Computer is God and Internet the Umbilical Cord." *www.thehindu.com*. N.p., 13 Nov. 2010. Web. 6 Dec. 2010.

Brittney Cudnik

A Lake Full of Lies

2010 Award for Excellence in Researched Writing

In this essay, the author makes an argument about the ways in which a collection of poems about the Susan Smith murders makes a sustained argument about stereotyping and society. The writer makes her case using both quotations from the poems and references to articles and features about the crime and its aftermath. In the second paragraph, the writer uses the word "we"; what effect does the use of this word have on the reader's relationship to the argument? There is one occasion where the writer uses block quotation; what effect does the use of longer direct quotation have on the reader? Why do you think the writer chose to directly quote this statement?

In a series of short poems, Cornelius Eady, the author of *Brutal Imagination,* retells the disturbing story of Susan Smith through the eyes of the imaginary "black man" that Smith created. Susan Smith killed her two sons by leaving them in the car while she let it roll into a lake; the two children drowned to death. Smith then went to the authorities and told them that an African American had hijacked her car and kidnapped her children. Eady takes the story that Smith created and retells it through the eyes of the man she created; he represents the idea of racial stereotypes of African Americans and the ignorance behind these stereotypes. Eady also makes connections between the stereotypes presented in Smith's story and stereotypical figures that are sociably acceptable in society.

As we read the poem "The Law," Eady connects those thoughts of the "black man" to racial assumptions about the African American. This shows us the "other side" of the story and voices the opinion of the African American race that is being misrepresented in Susan Smith's story. Eady's poem argues that, because he is a black man, no one will believe him innocent; the law will accept Susan's story that he entered her car when stopped at a traffic light. (Eady 16). Here the imagined voice is making the point that he will do whatever Smith creates him to. Yet in the end that does not matter; society and the authorities believed her false story until she was proven guilty. The historical legacy has determined it is more acceptable to believe that an African American has committed a crime, compared to a mother's doing so. A mother is viewed as a caring and loving figure, and someone who would do anything to protect their child, which makes Smith's story believable because society could not believe that she would commit the crime.

These stereotypes created in society make us biased in favor of the stories that people tell, or in Smith's case, create. We believe these stories because they are socially acceptable. In an article written after the confession of Susan Smith, William F. Buckley explains how it is easier to blame the African American race because of society's views. The article proves the point that as a society we did believe her story because of the societal assumption that African Americans are more likely to commit crimes, and that mothers would never do such a thing.

In chapter two of *Brutal Imagination,* Eady connects the Susan Smith case with stereotypical representations of the African American community, accepted media figures like Uncle Tom, Aunt Jemina, and Stepin Fetchit. By doing this, he supports the idea that Smith created her story because it could be socially acceptable. Eady connects Stepin Fetchit to the idea that it is okay to view African Americans a certain way. "There's only an image left that they/ Name you after, toothy, slow, / Worthy of a quick kick in the pants" (Eady 32). By referring to Stepin Fetchit Eady shows us that when an African American represented the stereotypical view, it is equally as bad as racial artifacts or stereotypical assumptions created by whites; the stereotype in this case is represented by a member of the stereotyped race. Eady wants to show us that this image of Stepin Fetchit shows a negative representation and influences us to believe that these stereotypes are okay, when in reality they are hurtful.

The idea that it is okay to accept some of these stereotypes is still present in the media. Even now, in 2010, there are racial artifacts in the media that represent hurtful and stereotypical beliefs about African Americans. Dr. Pilgrim, a professor at Ferris State University, has collected over 4,000 racial artifacts thoughout his life, even artifacts from recent years. He named his museum in honor of the Jim Crow Laws and the racial character created by Thomas Dartmouth Rice (*Jim Crow*). In the museum's website, Dr. John Thorp claims,

> "At the beginning of the 19th century, . . . [caricatures of African Americans] were consciously promoted to defend slavery. . . . into the 20th centuries, they served to justify the ongoing oppression of African-Americans. Their continuing reproduction underscores the bigotry and prejudice that must be overcome . . . to become a truly multicultural democracy" (*Jim Crow*).

This remark by Dr. Thorp underscores how the misrepresentation of African Americans through racial artifacts and misunderstood roles, like Jim Crow, helps society create and follow stereotypes about African Americans. While reading Eady's work we can agree that Eady connects the stereotypes on which Susan relies with stereotypes accepted in society.

In the final poem of *Brutal Imagination,* "Birthing," Eady combines Smith's confession with the "black man's" view, along with quotations from other people who expressed their opinion about the case. Here Eady represents the true voice of Smith and the underlying voice of the imaginary man Eady is representing. This poem indicates that Smith needed to create a believable story to hide her lies, and the story that would be most believable would be about an African American. Eady juxtaposes in this poem the voices of Smith and a black woman as well as that of the speaker, the imaginary black man, who states that on the day of the murders, he was no more than an idea in Smith's mind. Through this poem Eady is arguing that Smith knew the story she was creating, and didn't just pull it out of thin air. When the speaker says he is an "understanding" of Smith's, it connects with the idea of socially-accepted stereotypes. Eady also addresses the idea that people try to hide their racism and stereotypical beliefs, by claiming to be misunderstood or claiming ignorance. After the trial, a Smith family representative, Vaughn, quoted Smith to reporters: "On behalf of my family, I would like to apologize to the black community. It is really disturbing to think that this would be a racial issue. It is a terrible misfortune that all this happened" (Vobejda). Here Smith is expressing her ignorance about the situation she created; Smith is attempting to avoid blame by claiming her ignorance of the racial discrimination inherent in her story. Eady wants us to see that you cannot cover discrimination with ignorance, because it still affects the community that it discriminates against.

The idea that stereotypes and racial discrimination are present in society today is what Eady is trying to address in *Brutal Imagination*. Through the voice of the imagined "black man" Smith created, we can conclude that feigned ignorance of the stereotypical image society accepts significantly affects the community it is directed at—in this case, the African Americans. The message we should take from Eady's writing is that the more we blame others based on stereotypes, the more we judge people for something they are not. This leads us to living out our lives based on lies, just like the lies that Susan Smith told. So in the end we are all not experiencing the truth of each other; we are just swimming in a lake full of lies.

Works Cited

Buckley, William F., Jr. "Is everybody a racist?" *National Review* 19 Dec. 1994: 71. *General OneFile*. Web. 2 Mar. 2010.

Eady, Cornelius. *Brutal Imagination*. New York: G.P Putnam's Sons, 2001. Print.

Jim Crow: the Museum of Racist Memorabilia. Ferris State University, 1999. Web. 2 Mar. 2010. <http://www.ferris.edu/news/jimcrow/menu.htm>.

Vobejda, Barbara. "Smith's Kin Apologize To Blacks." *Washington Post* 9 Nov. 1994: A8. *Lexisnexis*. Web. 24 Feb. 2010.

First-Year Seminar Writing

Laurie Donati

Environmental Themes in Disney Films

2013 Honorable Mention for Excellence in First-Year Seminar Writing

Walt Disney films are known worldwide for memorable musical hits and morally righteous tales. However, in between catchy songs, environmental themes are prevalent in Disney's popular films *Bambi*, *The Lion King*, and *Pocahontas*. *Bambi* was released in 1942, *The Lion King* was released in 1994, and *Pocahontas* was released in 1995. Even though these movies were released at different times, the environment remains a crucial role in each of the films. While the three films are diverse in music and setting, all of the movies focus upon the idea of the circle of life. This reoccurring theme delivers the message that every living organism eventually will become part of the environment. The three films ultimately teach viewers to have a fundamental respect for nature. The use of music and realistic illustration in Disney's *Bambi*, *The Lion King*, and *Pocahontas* illuminates the importance of protecting and acknowledging the wonders of the environment.

The film *Bambi* is the first nature film by Disney that begins and ends with the recurring environmental theme of the circle of life. The first scene in *Bambi* depicts the birth of the new prince of the forest. All of the woodland animals gather around with excitement to witness the birth of Bambi because they know that he will someday be king. The community of woodland animals recognizes that eventually Bambi's parents will die and their offspring will rule the forest. Understanding the concept that a new life will replace death illustrates the never-ending circle of life. At the end of the film, the woodland animals once again gather around in anticipation to view the new prince of the forest. However, the prince now depicts Bambi's twin fawns. Likewise, the melody, "Love is a Song," that is heard during the opening credits in *Bambi* relates to the never-ending circle of life. The lyrics affirm that when a life ends, a new life and love will take its place. *Bambi*, the 1942 film that begins with the birth of Bambi and ends with the birth of Bambi's twin fawns, successfully illustrates that life inevitably continues forever.

The concept that life continues forever returns when Bambi's mother is murdered. The powerful, heart-breaking scene when Bambi's mother is shot and killed by a hunter has the greatest emotional impact on audiences worldwide. The scene takes place during the end of winter, causing Bambi's mother to mistakenly believe that the season's hardship was finally ending. However, the threat hunters pose to deer in the forest ultimately took her life instead of the tumultuous winter environment. Patricia Cohan, author of the article "Animated Bambi

Debate Arouses Pastoral Passions" (2008) states, "The anti-hunting message was conveyed on a completely emotional level through sympathy with its characters. It was targeted at children in their most impressionable, formative years" (Cohan 2008). Forming a bond with Bambi throughout the film causes viewers to feel grief-stricken when Bambi's mother dies because they know that she was his primary caregiver. Being exposed to Bambi's innocence and loving personality causes audience members to feel Bambi's confusion, sorrow, and anger when the sound of a gunshot is heard and his mother is left behind in the snow-covered forest. Realizing that humans inflict such devastating effects on wildlife through the eyes of Bambi has "inspired conservation awareness and laid the emotional groundwork for environmental activism" (Cohan 2008). The death of Bambi's mother communicates a strong anti-hunting message because viewers are able to see the pain through the perspective of a baby deer.

Moreover, the anti-hunting message appears even before Bambi's mother is tragically killed. When Bambi wants to play in an open meadow, his mother cautions him that even though the meadow is a beautiful place, it is very dangerous. Her caution against the meadow signifies how open areas in the environment pose a threat to an animal's safety because of hunters. The emphasis on hunting in the film *Bambi* serves as a tool to mold young minds into believing hunting is cruel to innocent animals.

Humans not only pose a detrimental threat to animals by hunting, they also cause forest fires. Near the end of *Bambi*, a forest fire ensues, awakening Bambi to the smell of smoke. Instantly, his father explains that the fire is the result of humans. Once again, humans are the root of all danger and destruction in the environment. By continuing to portray humans as the root of all evil it causes viewers to want to change their habits and protect the wonders of the environment.

In addition, the actual illustrations of the film are so realistic that it makes the issues of hunting and forest fires in various environments come to life for the audience. The artists who illustrated the deer and other forest animals in the film spent months observing and sketching deer and woodland life to make the illustrations accurate. By putting in the energy and time to make sure that the drawings were accurate representations of nature, viewers are able to build a stronger connection with the realistic characters. Having a connection with the animals in *Bambi* enables viewers to feel the urge to help protect wildlife. The 1942 film set a high standard for making natural, realistic animation by pursuing "the task of animating accurately the movements of four-legged deer as they walk, lie down, and get up, and of maintaining correct perspective for a rotating rack of antlers as a buck moves his head" (Lutts 1992*)*. Furthermore, the detailed representation of nature portrayed in Disney's *Bambi* allows viewers to build a bond with the woodland animals, ultimately persuading viewers to protect their environments so the animals can live in peace.

Fifty-two years after the release of *Bambi*, the film *The Lion King* hit theaters. Disney's *The Lion King* centers on the overarching theme of the circle of life. The most popular song of the film, "The Circle of Life," illustrates that death is not the end, but the beginning of a new life. The lyrics convey the theme of birth and the pursuit of making a change in the world. However a human, animal, or plant modifies its surroundings ultimately effects the natural environment and those living in the environment. A few scenes after the song "The Circle of Life" is heard, Mufasa, the king, brings his son Simba on a hunting lesson. He reveals to Simba, "The antelope may be food for lions, but when lions die, their bodies become the grass and essentially food for the antelope" (*The Lion King* Film). Mufasa's explanation of the circle of life successfully illustrates that every living thing, whether it be an animal or plant, becomes a part of the environment and of each other. Teaching Simba this life lesson proves how the environment unites all life, no matter how high up an organism is in the food chain.

The setting of each scene in *The Lion King* corresponds with the changing environment. The stampede alters the environment by stirring up the dirt and causing chaos, ultimately ending Mufasa's life. Before the stampede, Simba is practicing his roar and the atmosphere is calm and collective. A trembling pebble is shown at Simba's feet when the stampede is approaching, which is the beginning sign of a changing environment. The background music begins to intensify and become faster when the stampede ensues, which directly corresponds to the troubled atmosphere. In relation, the dusty, foggy air caused by the kicking of dirt in response to the stampede changes the entire mood of the scene, signifying danger and distress.

Similarly, the environment drastically changes when Scar, Mufasa's evil brother, becomes king after Mufasa's death. The rolling, vivid hills change to a barren open area where there is no food or livelihood. The obvious change in environment negatively impacts the animals' ability to survive in nature. When Nila and Simba reunite, she affirms that "there is no food, water, and soon enough we will all starve" (*The Lion King* Film). Viewing the desolate environment conveys the importance in protecting it because it is home to wildlife.

In 1995, Disney's *Pocahontas* was released. The award-winning song "Colors of the Wind" won both an Oscar and a Golden Globe for Best Original Song. The popularity of the song gave the film immense fame. The song continues the overarching theme of the circle of life as seen in *Bambi* and *The Lion King*. The melody gracefully conveys the idea that the environment connects everything in nature, uniting all organisms and natural resources as one. The lyrics perfectly reflect the theme of the circle of life. Pocahontas acknowledges that animals and humans should be friends, not enemies, because ultimately they are all connected. Her realization of the circle of life allows her to have a deep appreciation for the environment. The lyrics affirm Pocahontas's newfound gratitude for the beauty and richness of the environment. The poetic lyrics in "Colors of the Wind" successfully deliver the importance of protecting and recognizing the beauty and richness within every environment.

Walt Disney's three films, *Bambi*, *The Lion King*, and *Pocahontas* all focus upon the concept of the circle of life and the importance of not withholding the knowledge that every organism in nature is connected. The environmental messages in *Bambi* are conveyed through realistic illustration and emotional scenes that bring environmental issues of hunting and forest fires to light. *The Lion King* embraces environmental aspects through musical hits such as "The Circle of Life," dialogues, and drastic changes in scenery. The newest film that portrays elements of the environment depicts Disney's *Pocahontas*. The award-winning song "Colors of the Wind" effectively delivers the message to appreciate the environment and to have a beneficial relationship with the elements of nature. Through the use of music and realism, Disney's three successful films *Bambi*, *The Lion King*, and *Pocahontas* illustrate the importance in protecting and acknowledging the beauty of our environments.

Works Cited

Bambi. Dir. James Algar, Samuel Armstrong, David Hand, Graham Heid, Bill Roberts, Paul Satterfield, and Norman Wright. Perf. Hardie Albright, Stan Alexander, and Bobette Audrey. Walt Disney Productions. 1942. Film.

Cohan, Patricia. "Animated Bambi Debate Arouses Pastoral Passions." *The New York Times*. 23 Apr. 2008, Web. 3 Apr 2012. <www.nytimes.com/2008/04/23/Books/23bambi.html>.

King, Margaret J. "The Audience in the Wilderness." *Journal of Popular Film & Television* 24.2 (1996): 60.

The Lion King. Dir. Roger Allers and Rob Minkoff. Perf. Matthew Broderick, Jeremy Irons, and James Earl Jones. Walt Disney Pictures. 1994. Film.

Lutts, Ralph H. "The Trouble with Bambi: Walt Disney's Bambi and the American vision of Nature." *Forest and Conservation History* 36 (Oct 1992): 160–171.

Pocahontas. Dir. Mike Gabriel and Eric Goldberg. Perf. Mel Gibson, Linda Hunt, and Christian Bale. Walt Disney Pictures. 1995. Film.

Robertson, Duncan. "Bambi and Other Disney Characters are the 'Unsung Heroes of the Green Lobby' says Cambridge Academic" *Mail Online*. 25 Mar. 2008, Web. 3 Apr. 2012. <www .dailymail.co.uk/news/article-544229/Bambi-Disney-characters-unsung-heroes-green-lobby-says-Cambridge-academic.html>.

Samuel Perkins

Conversion Attempts and Results by the Christian Churches in Europe and America

2012 Award for Excellence in First-Year Seminar Writing

Perkins deftly weaves art historical analysis with historical and comparative religion criticism and commentary in one well-written package. Rembrandt and Bernini, he points out, are archetypes of these periods, but Perkins digs below the surface, revealing complexity, imperfection, point of view, and political motive behind the images, which he includes in the paper. This work demonstrates depth and breadth of knowledge, making connections between old- and new-world values and practices, art and politics.

1. The Differing Styles of Rembrandt and Bernini

Before the Protestant Reformation, Christianity had been united under the single banner of the Roman Catholic Church. However, during the Renaissance, many Christians had come to believe that the Roman Catholic Church had gone off of the righteous path. These malcontents began talking about starting their own church, separate from the Catholic Church. There were several separatist movements that sprang off from the Catholic Church during the Reformation, and collectively they were called the Protestant Churches. These Protestant sects placed more importance on piety, simple living, and hard work than the Catholic Church did.

In response to the Protestant Reformation, the Catholic Church launched a campaign dubbed "The Counter-Reformation" in which the church tried to persuade or scare the Christian people of Europe to rejoin the ranks of the Catholic Church. Art became one of the main tools used by both sides during the Reformation and the Counter-Reformation to win the loyalty of the Christian people of Europe. There were two artists at this time that really embodied the spirit of these two religious movements. The works of Rembrandt show the Reformed style, which was much more representational, while the works of Bernini show the Counter-Reformation style, which was more grandiose, domineering, and idealistic. The fundamental differences between these two styles show the different values that were viewed as important by members of the Protestant Churches and the Roman Catholic Church.

Rembrandt was born in the Protestant Netherlands and was raised a Calvinist (one of the several Protestant sects throughout Europe), went to school to be an artist, and mastered it by the time he was twenty-two (Kren and Marx 2012a). His Calvinist religion influenced the way he viewed the events in the Bible, and this view translated directly to his work as a predominantly religious artist. Bernini, on the other hand, was born in Catholic Italy and was raised a staunch Catholic. Bernini was eventually commissioned by Pope Paul V to produce religious works of art for the Vatican. Because of this commission, Bernini had to move to Rome (Kren and Marx 2012b). His Catholic upbringing and his proximity to the center of the Roman Catholic Church drastically influenced Bernini as an artist, and this influence was seen in his finished works.

Rembrandt took a different approach to painting images from the Bible than had been taken in the past. Rembrandt tried to paint scenes from the Bible in a very realistic, and European, way. Take, for example, his painting of *The Holy Family* (1630). In this painting, the holy family is shown as just a regular family, and none of them have halos around their heads. Religious figures had always been painted with halos around their heads before this, which is why this painting is a great example of the Reformed style. The Protestant churches wanted to make the holy family a unit that the average European could relate to instead of being terrified of (*Art and the Bible* 2005). The setting of this painting is in what appears to be a Dutch workshop of some kind, and the holy family appears to be in northern European peasantry outfits. This is interesting because the holy family actually was from Israel, and Jesus was born in a manger, not a workshop.

Rembrandt also depicted Jesus as an actual person, instead of depicting him as a superior and perfect being. Take his painting of *Christ on the Cross* (1640) as an example. Earlier Christian artists' depictions of Jesus showed him with a halo around his head and an emotionless expression on his face. Rembrandt's depiction of Jesus in this painting shows him without the halo and with intense emotion across his face (Prusak 2012:9). This image of Jesus' execution on the cross evokes feelings of sadness and pity from the viewer, while earlier Christian (and later Counter-Reformation) depictions of Christ on the cross were really meant to remind the viewer what Jesus did for them and evoke a feeling of obligation. This action of trying to relate these holy figures from the Bible to the common people was a very Protestant idea, and this is why Rembrandt's paintings are all realistic and simple in style.

Most of Bernini's sculptures focused on religious figures, but, since he painted in the Counter-Reformation style, many of Bernini's depictions of religious events and figures are grandiose or domineering. One of the most famous examples of Counter-Reformation art was the sculpture *The Ecstasy of St. Theresa* (1652). This sculpture depicts the death of St. Theresa and her being lifted up to Heaven by an angel. The two figures in this sculpture are obviously considered holy figures, as the rays of heavenly light behind them successfully displays. *The Ecstasy of St. Theresa* is an awe-inspiring piece of work; people would stop and be amazed by what they saw, which is exactly what the Counter-Reformation was trying to do (White 2000).

Another one of Bernini's works, *The Crucified Christ* (1655), shows the domineering side of the Counter-Reformation style. In this sculpture Jesus is on the cross with his head hanging down toward the ground. The body of Jesus is chiseled exquisitely, but there is not much focus on the face. Also, the nails that are driven through Jesus' hands and feet have left no blood trails. Bernini was great at depicting the body through sculpture, but was not very adept at conveying intense emotion through this medium (Standring 2008). This clean and emotionless Jesus makes the work less personal, portraying him as a perfect figure and not as an actual human being; a figure to worship, not relate to.

The differences between Rembrandt's work and Bernini's work are vast and offer a glimpse into the conflicting ideologies of the Protestant Churches and the Roman Catholic Church at the time of the Reformation. The Protestant Churches wanted to make religion and religious figures accessible to the common people so they could follow their own path to righteousness. The Catholic Church wanted to fill the people with feelings of fear and awe so that they would continue to listen to local priest and the decrees of the Catholic Church (Survey of Western Art). Thus, since he was a member of one of the Protestant Churches, Rembrandt's work is much more realistic and filled with a sense of humanity than Bernini's. Since Bernini was Roman Catholic and commissioned by the Pope, most of his works are grandiose and domineering.

The battle over the souls of the Christian faith would continue until the beginning stages of the Industrial Revolution, when national identity would become significantly more important than religious affiliation in determining one's allies and enemies. However, the works of art produced by this period of religious strife are still admired and studied in modern-day circles of art specialists. This is because those works of art help us understand the main differences between the two sides during this time, and we can use this to understand the major wars that erupted during the Reformation. We can then see how this religious conflict of the Renaissance still influences the world, which leads us to a better understanding of modern issues in today's world.

2. A Whole Different Perspective on Christian Religion: Native American Christianity

When Christopher Columbus "discovered" America in 1492, he opened up the gates for a massive wave of colonization, disease, and Christianity to flood the new world and forever change it. Europeans came to the new world so that they could become rich and to convert the Native population to Christianity. The different nationalities and religious sects handled the conversion of the Native Americans in different ways, but this was one of the main cornerstones of all colonization plans. Natives were often forced to abandon their traditional religions and convert to Christianity by the greater European powers. Even the United States participated in the conversion of Native tribes on the plains and the west coast, although this occurred much after earlier conversions. Catholic and Protestant attempts to convert the Native population of the Americas to Christianity had very mixed results. The Natives that did convert would eventually infuse Christianity with aspects of their traditional religions and grow to dislike many other Christians and even the term itself because of the forceful conversion.

Different nationalities and religious sects tried to convert the Natives of the Americas in different ways. The Spanish Catholics were extremely zealous when it came to converting the Natives. Most of these Natives had been enslaved by the Spanish and worked on sugar plantations or in mines. As part of their enslavement, most Native slaves were forced to convert to Catholicism by their masters (Saito 2006:172). The Catholic Church in New Spain designed their churches on an extremely grandiose scale so that the Natives could be awed by the power of God (see figure 1). These churches were even more extravagant inside, with the main altarpiece being made out of gold in some cases (see figure 2). This extravagance was meant to show how powerful God was when compared to the Natives and how, because of this, he should be worshiped by them. The French Catholics in modern-day Canada approached the conversion of Natives differently. The French colonists did not enslave the Native populations but instead traded with them for furs. Catholic missionaries would usually spend some time in a Native tribe with the traders where they would try to convert the Natives to Catholicism. The French approach, however, was not very effective, and not many converts were won (Seed 1995:186).

The Protestant English had an even harder time converting the Natives than the French did. The Puritans tried to convert Native populations on the south and north shores of Massachusetts, but failed. After the failed attempts at conversion, squabbles over land erupted into a great war between the English and the Massachusetts Natives called King Phillip's War. After the war, the English believed that it was impossible to convert the Natives until they were "civilized" (Bragg 2000:5–6). Thus, the English began a policy of destroying Native groups whenever they moved into a new area or trying to bring them into English culture, and not many converts were won. In the nineteenth century the United States of America tried to convert the Natives in the plains and west coast of North America by placing them on reservations where they were encouraged to farm and convert to Christianity. However, this approach did not work very well because many of the Natives had a hard time learning to farm and flat out refused to convert to Christianity (Nebraska Studies n.d.). Thus, reservations became a dumping ground for Natives by the American government. These Natives on reservations were primarily fed by government rations because they never learned to farm.

The Natives who did convert to Christianity were mostly centered in Central and South America with a few other tribes in the American west. Before European contact, Native populations had created their own religious practices that were very similar to Christianity in form. These practices included creation myths, an all-powerful spiritual deity, and specially trained spiritual leaders in the community (Heyrman 2012:1). These similarities made the transition from Native religions to Christianity pretty simple because the Natives were really changing the Deity that they worshiped. However, the Natives did change Christianity to fit their own world view better. Many Natives refer to God as "the Creator" instead of "my Lord" because they dislike the connection of the word "Lord" with slavery. Also, the congregations that worship in the Christian reservations in western America participate in many non-Christian activities such as attending sweats, sun dances, and placing sacred pipes on the altar next to the bread and wine (Roller n.d.). There are also many examples of Native Christian art made on the western Christian reservations. Figure 3 shows the Virgin Mary in a classic pose, but she is Native American dressed in a Native outfit instead of being the traditional Caucasian figure dressed in medieval garb. This painting shows that Native Christians are identifying with Christianity and placing their own culture into the stories (Dockstader 1994:2).

Although many Native Americans are technically Christian by definition (which is a person who believes that Christ died and was resurrected), they refuse to identify themselves as Christians. For many Native Americans the term "Christian" reminds them of the civilizations that came in and destroyed their way of life. The people who identified themselves as Christians in the past (Conquistadors, Puritans, and several American army officers) ended up declaring war on different Native tribes and enslaved, destroyed, or forced the Native populations off their lands (Roller n.d.). Many Native Christians see a distinct difference between what the Christian religion preaches, which is to tolerate different views and treat others the same way you want to be treated, and what the Christians actually did to the Native populations, which was to destroy an entire culture and force the people of that culture to assimilate. Many Native Christians do not want to be called Christians because of the negative association that the term has with a violent history.

3. Evangelization Attempts by Catholics and Protestants in Europe and America

The differences between the ways the Christian Churches tried to convert Europeans and then, later, the Native Americans is very interesting. During the Reformation, Protestant artists tried to depict the Holy Family as a relatable unit while the Catholic Church depicted Holy figures as grandiose and unrelatable to keep people pious and wanting to worship the figures depicted. In America, the Catholic Church used its grandiose style of religious art to convert the Native populations in Central and South America. The Protestants who came to America had very little success with converting the Native populations, and so they gave up trying to convert the Natives and instead began moving Native populations off their land and placing European settlements there. Because the Protestants largely gave up trying to convert the Native populations, there is almost no religious art in the Reformed style aimed at converting the Natives. The Catholics in Central America used the Counter-Reformation style to convert the Natives there, but the Protestant colonists just began destroying Native villages, so they did not waste time and effort in creating religious art to convert the Natives.

When the United States began putting western Native Americans in reservations, they also began trying to convert them to Christianity. America is a largely Protestant country, so most of the missionaries that the Natives on the reservations met were members of different Protestant churches. As a result of this, most of the Native Americans on the reservations are Protestant Christians. The art that these Native Christians are producing actually slightly resembles the art that the Protestants were creating during the European Reformation. The Native Holy figures in these paintings are shown as normal people (see figure 3), which was one of the key things that identified the Reformed style of religious art.

The art styles that came out of the Protestant Reformation and the Catholic Counter-Reformation not only had a great impact on the populations of Europe but also on the Native populations of America. Many of the Catholic churches in Central and South America were and still are built in the Counter-Reformation grandiose style, which shows the impact that this form of Renaissance European art has had on the everyday life of modern-day Central and South Americans. The Native Christians on the reservations are producing art that shares similarities with the Protestant Reformed style. This is because these Natives were converted to Christianity by American Protestants who were familiar with the Reformed style of art from the Protestant Reformation. It is very interesting to see that art created during the Renaissance in Europe still heavily influences art in the modern day American continents.

Images

Rembrandt Van Rijn, The Holy Family (1630)

http://artoutthewazoo.com/2011/12/13/christmas-celebration-the-holy-family-in-western-art/

Rembrandt Van Rijn, Christ on the Cross (1640)

http://rembrandt.louvre.fr/en/html/r11.html

Bernini, The Ecstasy of St. Theresa (1652)

www.students.sbc.edu/oneal08/St.%20Theresa%20in%20Ecstasy.html

Bernini, The Crucified Christ: Bernini (1655)

www.ago.net/agoid102750

Figure 1 Church of San Miguel

Figure 2 Altar of San Miguel
Church

Figure 3 Native Mary

Works Cited

Art and the Bible. N.p., 16 July 2005. Web. 22 Feb. 2012.

Baroque Art. Survey of Western Art, 5 Jan. 2001. Web. 22 Feb. 2012.

Bragg, Chad. "Missions to Native Americans." *North American Missions.org*. Ed. J. D. Pain. North American Missions.org, 2000. Web. 29 Mar. 2012.

Dockstader, Frederick. "Native American art." *History.com*. History Channel, 1994. Web. 29 Mar. 2012.

Heyrman, Christine Leigh. "Native American Religion in Early America." Divining America, TeacherServe®. National Humanities Center. 29 Mar. 2012.

Kren, Emil, and Daniel Marx. "Rembrandt van Rijn: Biography and Chronology." *Web Gallery of Art*. Ed. Emil Kren and Daniel Marx. N.p., 6 Apr. 2005. Web. 22 Feb. 2012a.

Kren, Emil, and Daniel Marx. "Bernin, Gian Lorenzo: Biography." *Web Gallery of Art*. Ed. Emil Kren and Daniel Marx. N.p., 13 Feb. 2006. Web. 22 Feb. 2012b.

NebraskaStudies.org. Nebraska State Historical Society, n.d. Web. 29 Mar. 2012.

Prusak, Bernard G. "The Moment of Recognition." *Commenweal* 16 (Dec. 2011): 8–12. *Academic OneFile*. Web. 22 Feb. 2012.

Roller, Julia. *Native and Christian*. Ed. Julia Roller. N.p., n.d. Web. 29 Mar. 2012.

Saito, Akira. "Art and Christian Conversion in the Jesuit Missions on the Spanish South American Frontier." *National Museum of Ethnology* (2006):171–201. Web. 29 Mar. 2012.

Seed, Patricia. *Ceremonies of Possession in Europe's Conquest of the New World, 1492–1640*. New York: Cambridge University Press, 1995. N. pag. Print.

Standring, Timothy J. "Marble made flesh: The Getty Museum is staging the first-ever exhibition devoted to Bernini's portrait busts. It reveals how triumphantly he succeeded in his aim to 'express what one goes on in the heads of heroes'." *Apollo* Oct. 2008: 108+. *Academic OneFile*. Web. 22 Feb. 2012.

Stone, Matt. *Glocal Christianity*. Ed. Matt Stone. Glocal Christianity, 2004. Web. 29 Mar. 2012.

White, Veronica. "Gian Lorenzo Bernini (1598–1680)". In *Heilbrunn Timeline of Art History*. New York: The Metropolitan Museum of Art, 2000–. www.metmuseum.org/toah/hd/bern/hd_bern.htm (October 2003)

Michael A. Verlezza

Context and Significance:
A Primary Source Document Analysis

2011 Award for Excellence in First-Year Seminar Writing

This essay, written for a First Year Seminar, demonstrates a real understanding of the context and significance of the journal article the writer is analyzing. Notice how the essay's writer makes clear the historic context for the article—just a month before the first Stanley Cup; geographically, too, the writer places the article in the Northeast US and notes how the author of the article calls his own nationality into question by identifying with Canadian hockey-lovers. This sort of analysis, where the writer must demonstrate the relationship of a primary text to the area being covered in a class, is not uncommon. This writer has provided a very graceful response to the challenge and makes an informative case for the importance of the document being analyzed. Notice how the writer interweaves historical information and rhetorical analysis in his discussion of the article.

Less than two decades after the advent of ice hockey in Montreal, Charles Gordon Rogers published his magazine article "A Championship Hockey Match in Canada" in the American sports magazine *Outing*. This essay will investigate Rogers' mission and message in his appeal to swell the ranks of the hockey faithful. The content of his article was appropriate, given the title he selected. At its core it was a dramatic and impassioned recounting of a championship hockey game in 1894. While Rogers is prone to hyperbole, he managed nicely to encapsulate appropriately the back-and-forth of the game, the endless boredom and anticipation of intermission, and the thrill that followed the victorious home team.

The article commences with a description of the venue along with the expectant crowd. After negotiating the box office and the "eager endeavor to secure tickets" (409), the author explains how the crowd grew impatient as the designated start time of the game came and went. Rogers follows with his description of the two teams. The author describes the noticeably less popular visiting champions and their challengers, the naturally preferred home team. Rogers specifically lauds the home team's cover point and right wing, explaining that the latter is "a Hercules of muscle, but as fair in play as King Arthur in the lists of Camelot" (410). Thereafter Rogers outlines his expectations for the advancement of both hockey and lacrosse and how they might someday supplant baseball in popularity in his native United States. Following this, the contest begins in earnest, and there is a description of the actual play by play of the match. He describes in detail how, despite scoring first, the champion visitors ultimately found themselves behind by a score four to one. They fought on valiantly and added another score of their own, but at the final whistle, the fans stormed the rink and the home team was crowned victorious.

Rogers does not identify the specific game that has been played, which renders any attempt to verify an accurate recounting of the game impossible. According to one source though, a review of the box scores from the 1894 season of the Amateur Hockey Association of Canada shows no games with a final score of 4–2 (Worldlingo.com). The reader is nonetheless left with the feeling of what it was like to be present at such an event. The author describes tense-ness in the air prior to the game as men pursued tickets to the event, for example. What is most striking, however, is Rogers' sensationalist writing style. The amateur ideal was alive and well in Canadian sport at the end of the 1800s, and the author made it a point to compare the players to some of the most celebrated warriors and artists in history. To this end, both King Arthur and Hector are mentioned by name, as are Machiavelli and Polish Prime Minis-ter (and celebrated pianist) Ignacy Jan Paderewski. This noble ideal stands in stark contrast to what Gruneau and Whitson call the "unapologetically commercial" (66) culture of baseball. Gruneau and Whitson further reinforce the appropriateness of Rogers' metaphors for the era: "the quality of a team's performance actually said something about the community that pro-duced it . . . about the character of its people" (67). In this way we see that the players were not entirely dissimilar from Hector and Achilles as they too were the anointed representatives of their cities.

From 1891 to 1896, Charles Gordon Rogers wrote an array of articles for *Outing* magazine on a diverse range of subjects. The magazine itself was published by two separate compa-nies, initially in Albany and later by the Wheelman Company in Boston. The locality of these publishing companies tells us that the intended audience for *Outing* magazine (and therefore Rogers' article) would have been the American Northeast—specifically New England and upstate New York. Rogers alludes to this distribution himself when he pleads for the international dissemination of hockey "so far as the border cities and those cities of the great republic where good ice can be had" (410). Given that hockey in this era was still typically limited to middle-class white amateurs and given the additional understanding that one must be literate to consume a magazine article, we can further conclude that individuals of that demographic would have been the specific audience for Rogers' entry in *Outing*. It is also important to note that Rogers specifically explains that men of all ages and even young women were in attendance at the hockey game. This indicates to us that Rogers subscribed to the notion that the game was accepting of female spectators, even if it would not neces-sarily be appropriate for women to play the game themselves. His adoption of this position would have then paved the way for the aforementioned middle-class white men to secure the approval of their wives and for young women to contribute to the game as spectators.

As Canada and the US approached the final decade of the nineteenth century, more atten-tion was paid to leisure. In a striated society that incorporated the working class and the super-rich, there emerged a clear middle class. This new middle class found themselves away from their employers for more hours per day than ever before. Consequently, a spate of activities emerged to vie for their time and discretionary income. Chief among them were the nickelodeons and athletic activities which were widely varied along geographic lines. In Rogers' homeland the United States, for example, "Major League Baseball's attendance expanded from 3.6 million to over nine million between 1900 and 1920. Estimates are that softball playing increased even more rapidly" (Fischer, par. 7). Naturally there was a desire to tap into this market as it emerged.

Rogers' bias was driven precisely by that desire. As a witness of high-caliber play, he felt a specific ownership of the game and as such was compelled to sell it to nonbelievers. In this way he was a hockey evangelist, spreading the word of hockey across his targeted geographic area. While he advocated for the game, he raised questions of his own citizenship and included himself in the Canadian collective by saying "we in Canada" (Rogers 410). In this same section he also mentioned his "native land" and his concerns of becoming a "prophet without honor" as he explained his expectations for the Nordic sports to overthrow baseball in a swell of popular demand. The author concluded his sale of the game with the following: "It is a 'roaring' game, and as regards Canada there need be no uncertain feeling as to its longevity" (Rogers 410).

Outing was published in the backyard of the birthplace of baseball and would have used articles like Rogers' to help readers fill the void in spectator sports that existed in wintertime. There existed tremendous social pressure to participate in "the obsessive concern for manliness in sporting competition" (Gruneau and Whitson 67). Rogers participated, not by playing necessarily, but by selling the game to *Outing* who in turn sold the game to its readers. Here we can clearly identify the conflict of interest between the commercialization of the game of hockey and the high esteem in which the amateur game was held.

"A Championship Hockey Match in Canada" is notable, specifically given the timeframe during which it was published. The Stanley Cup was first awarded on March 17, 1894, and this particular issue of *Outing* was published in February of that same year. While his article predated that year's championship game between the Montreal Hockey Club and the Ottawa Generals, Rogers still captured the feelings which those at the Victoria Skating Rink must have felt on that day. Additionally, the article helps us appreciate the stock that was placed in the acumen of local teams through the lionization of local talent. Finally and most importantly, we can point to Rogers' article and see in it direct correlations to today's game.

Works Cited

"1894 AHAC season." *WorldLingo.com*. N.p., 4 June 2010. Web. 22 Sept. 2010. <http://www.worldlingo
.com/ma/enwiki/en/1894_AHAC_season>.

Fischer, Claude S. "Changes in Leisure Activities, 1890–1940." *Journal of Social History* 22 Mar.
1994. Web. 19 Sept. 2010. <http://www.highbeam.com/doc/1G1-15324637.html>.

Gruneau, Richard, and David Whitson. *Hockey Night in Canada: Sport, Identities and Cultural Politics*. Toronto: Garamond Press, 1993. Print.

Rogers, Charles G. "A Championship Hockey Match in Canada." *Outing* 23.5 (1894): 409–11. Web.
18 Sept. 2010.

Fiona Steacy

Robert Mapplethorpe

2010 Award Winner for Excellence in First-Year Seminar Writing

In this essay, the author offers a discussion of the controversies surrounding the work of the artist Robert Mapplethorpe. Notice how the author acknowledges the elements of Mapplethorpe's work which may offend some, but maintains a clear claim that Mapplethorpe's work, although disturbing, is an artistic expression of a subculture. College essays often require the writer to take a stance on a subject about which informed opinion differs. Notice the variety of this writer's sources. How well do you feel this writer has supported her position?

Robert Mapplethorpe was a photographer whose work has garnered both high praise and harsh criticism. His photographs range from innocuous pictures of flowers to striking nudes to blunt depictions of unusual sexual acts. Mapplethorpe has been criticized, generally by a conservative audience, for the homoeroticism, racial fetishism, and sadomasochism that are, to varying degrees, graphically represented in his work. Though many of Mapplethorpe's photographs are blatantly and purposely shocking, they are also valid works of art that celebrate the beauty of the human form and depict a taboo sexual subculture with a singular, disturbing frankness.

One of the more predictable controversies surrounding Mapplethorpe's work concerns the graphic nature of his photographs. *Double Fist Fuck* is a photograph from *Pictures*, a compilation of his work. It shows two fists inserted into a man's anus. Undeniably, images such as this one are arrestingly explicit and perhaps even nauseating for some. Camille Paglia, in her response to Mapplethorpe critic Rochelle Gurstein, agrees that the attempts of so-called "experts" trying to "aestheticize intentionally shocking content are . . . 'insults to common sense'" (43). However, Paglia believes that such attempts detract from the integrity of the work, whereas Gurstein does not see Mapplethorpe's work as ever having possessed any integrity. Though the photographs of sadomasochistic sexual acts are unusual and sometimes gruesome, they are nonetheless art. Some might describe them as purely "sensational," but they are meant to do more than just shock. Mapplethorpe's subjects are depicted with a gritty realism, in a way that one might consider almost educational: the photographs unabashedly expose viewers to a dark side of sex that involves pain, humiliation, and yet, somehow, pleasure. Mapplethorpe himself claims that he discovered things about his own sexuality through taking photographs. "It was as though I wasn't documenting anything but myself in a way" (*Pictures*).

Though there is no doubt that Mapplethorpe wanted to shock his audiences, it seems that he also wanted them to be aware of the underground activities that occur on the fringes of American society.

In addition to sadomasochistic practices, Mapplethorpe's sexual photographs often included homosexuality. As a gay man, Mapplethorpe's goal with these images was likely to present a subject with which he was familiar and in which he felt personally invested. These homoerotic images were often displayed alongside his photographs of sadomasochism, linking the two topics. In 1989, an exhibition of a variety of Mapplethorpe's work was scheduled to be shown in the Corcoran Gallery of Art, but following protests from organizations like the American Family Association, it was cancelled. Since the show was to receive funding from the National Endowment for the Arts, many Americans were upset that their own money was being used to support art that they did not condone (Quigley). Though no single reason was given for the cancellation, the gay and lesbian protests that ensued suggest that the depiction of homosexuality was a major factor. This censorship of the arts is a restriction of freedom. If Americans wish to support art at all, they must accept that controversial works, such as Mapplethorpe's homoerotic images, have as much a right to funding as do agreeable works.

Mapplethorpe's photographs sometimes exclusively feature black males, as in his *Black Book*. This has been perceived, by a wide variety of people, to be exploitative. According to Kobena Mercer, a gay black man, Mapplethorpe's "pornographic" nudes perpetuate "a whole range of racist myths about black sexuality" (Mercer 463). Mercer and others believe that these images of black male nudes objectify their subjects, portraying them only as sexual "things." Mapplethorpe's racial fetishism, they claim, is evident in the way he emphasizes the genitalia and occasionally crops the heads of the men (465). However, Mapplethorpe's works are more a simple appreciation of the black male form than a conscious attempt to sexualize black men and reinforce stereotypes. His 1982 portrait, *Jimmy Freeman*, shows a naked man, crouched, with his head bowed. The man's penis is distinctly visible, yet he is not provocatively posed (Fig. 1). Though the prominent genitals may appear to be exploitative when taken out of context, in the photograph, they seem a natural component of the man's general physical flawlessness. The title of the work, which is the subject's name, also introduces a personal element. With this title, Mapplethorpe acknowledges that, although the man is depicted as only a beautiful thing, outside the photograph he is more than just an object.

Throughout his career, photographer Robert Mapplethorpe composed a large body of work. Though some of his pieces are uncontroversial, many of them have caused conflict with their sexual themes. Despite their intentionally shocking nature, these photographs are valuable works of art that shamelessly present their subjects. Though Mapplethorpe is now deceased, the divisive topics of sex, race, and homosexuality depicted in his work will remain controversial for years to come.

Works Cited

Estate of Robert Mapplethorpe. *Pictures*. Ed. Dimitri Levas. New York: Distributed Art Publishers, 1999. Print.

Mercer, Kobena. "Robert Mapplethorpe and the Fantasies of Race." *Feminism and Pornography*. Ed. Drucilla Cornell. New York: Oxford University Press, 2000. 460–75. Print.

Paglia, Camille. *Sex, Art, and American Culture*. New York: Random House, 1992. Print.

Quigley, Margaret. "The Mapplethorpe Censorship Controversy." *Publiceye.org*. Political Research Associates, 2008. Web. 14 December 2009.

Second-Year Seminar Writing

Amy Pistone

The Silence of Happily-Ever-After

2013 Honorable Mention for Excellence in Second-Year Seminar Writing

Silence is not created equal. Sometimes it is used as a form of oppression, to strip individuals of verbal communication as a form of punishment. Other times, silence can bring liberation of those oppressed individuals, allowing a silent protest. Specifically, the silence of *women* has been illustrated in film to demonstrate the issue of control, or lack thereof, among females. In Jane Campion's *The Piano* and Disney's *The Little Mermaid*, women's silence is utilized as a tool to represent patriarchal society and how it affects the autonomy of women. While these two films share some commonalities, as will be discussed later, the depiction of "voluntary" female silence is shown to be starkly different. It is important to note that the films were released within four years of each other, with *The Little Mermaid* in 1989, and *The Piano* in 1993, yet they offer strangely different portrayals of women and their relationships with silence. It is clear through a close analysis of Campion's film that womanly silence is represented as a form of empowerment, and thus *The Piano* is a strictly feminist piece. In contrast, Disney's rendition of *The Little Mermaid* demonstrates voluntary silence as a loss of control and surrender to patriarchal society in a piece that is decidedly unfeminist.

The silence of both of the lead females in each film can be considered to be voluntary, an important quality worthy of discussion. In the opening voiceover, Ada is said to have suddenly ceased all verbal communication at the age of six, for a reason she does not know, but it is her "will," a self-imposed silence. Yet she can clearly communicate through other modes, which is the key difference in comparison to Ariel. Kimberly Chabot Davis states this idea clearly: "Although Ada is silent, she has other outlets such as gesture, writing, and music to communicate meaning and deep feeling" (Davis 2007:72). Furthermore, throughout the course of the film, various sounds are slightly audible from her—a shocked gasp or a pleased moan, which demonstrates that she has the ability to verbally communicate to some extent, yet she has abstained from doing so. On the other hand, Ariel is shown happily chirping away to Flounder in shipwrecks, singing her heart out in her grotto, and scolding Sebastian for most of the first portion of the film. However, she voluntarily signs her voice away to Ursula for a chance to win the heart of her Prince, which is problematic for many reasons. As stated previously, Ada's silence is not really a pure silence in that she still has an ability to communicate, while Ariel does not. In comparison, Ariel is left floundering around on land with the lack of her voice and is not shown to be able to communicate with Prince Eric. She had no outlet to represent her needs and feelings, which starts to show the negative consequences of her actions and the actual problems with her silence. While it is now clear that both women have employed this silence on a purely voluntary basis, the issue of control must be discussed to highlight the key differences that make the films worthy of feminist discussion.

The idea of female control is the crucial element in distinguishing the two films, as well as in declaring *The Piano* to be feminist and *The Little Mermaid* anti-feminist. First, the fact that Ada has these other outlets of communication proves that she does have a sense of control of her own life. Her silence is a form of empowerment, as no other person is successfully able to demand anything of her, and instead she is shown to defiantly stare down others who challenge her, most notably her husband Alistair Stewart. As Davis writes, "[feminists] who felt that Ada's silence was purposive usually saw it as a powerful feminist gesture, but they emphasized either her silence or her alternative voice" (74). However, *both* of these attributes are necessary in evaluating Ada's sense of control. Her silence speaks volumes as she stands in comparison to the other females in the film; she is not concerned with mere gossip. Rather, Ada's silence is important in that she is unapologetic for it; she does not view it to be a flaw of hers and for the majority of the film, she does not actively try to become more verbal. Accordingly, her alternative voice of her piano is just as important because it suggests a deeper meaning of communication, something that she is striving hard to express in a more stylistic form. Thus, Ada is seen pouring her emotions into each musical piece, showing her lustful and loving feelings toward Baines. Likewise, her gestures and body language express her control when she dictates how many keys she demands in return for compliance to Baines' desires, or her refusal to bend to Stewart's. Conversely, Ariel's silence implies a loss of control. For one, the decision to give up her voice implicitly shows a loss, because she must give up her talent to gain her legs. As Laura Sells writes, "Even more disheartening, she purchases this physical transformation with her voice" (Sells 1995:179). But one could also question the idea that Ariel's silence was voluntary. In actuality, Ariel's voice is being forcibly taken away from her by Ursula in exchange for what the mermaid yearns for: a man. While she exhibits strong desires to leave the ocean, it is the fact that Eric is the catalyst for her decision to trade her voice that is problematic, because Ariel is losing her ability to communicate in order to gain love. Consider one of the key parallels between the films: the inclusion of musical talent among the ladies. Ada's aptitude and love for the piano is shown cohesively throughout the film, without question it is a part of her soul that she utilizes to demonstrate her control as well as her emotions, while Ariel's talent for singing is clearly displayed at the start of the film and then vanishes as her voice does and she is left passively sitting along for the remaining musical numbers, showing her absence of autonomy.

Regardless of the how silence manifests itself within the women, both films use silence as a response to patriarchy, albeit in different ways. Ada is shown to be actively reacting to the patriarchy in virtually every way. While the system attempts to oppress her, she fights against it. Her silence is her weapon against the patriarchy, or her form of gaining control in a world that is trying to take her voice away. By refusing to speak, she is demanding that the men listen to her. The audience sees Ada stomp away during wedding photos for an arranged marriage that she refuses to actually take part in, the audible ripping of a wedding dress suggesting a metaphorical tearing of patriarchal expectation. She controls the husband that she does not wish to have, even as he is shown struggling in vain to keep the power over her. A sharp smack of her hand across Baines' face ends with a ringing silence of clarity in which he must acknowledge Ada's autonomy. She returns for him when she is not obligated to anymore, and she does not allow him to misinterpret her feelings. Even in the worst circumstances, Ada refuses to let patriarchy have any sort of hold over her. On a dreary day, Stewart cuts off her finger in a fit of rage in an effort to silence her. No loud cries of pain are heard, just a low murmur as she cradles her hand, almost in disbelief that he would attempt to do such a thing, and still she will not allow any man to force any reaction out of her. A close-up shot of her eyes stops Stewart in his tracks during his attempted rape of Ada. She does not need to verbally express that this is wrong; all she needs is her conviction and inner strength to halt a man from overpowering her. Her silence speaks volumes.

On the other hand, patriarchy actively oppresses Ariel and her voluntary silence only furthers this and results in the absence of autonomy. After she signs her voice away, she is no longer the fiery girl who explores shipwrecks and swims away from sharks. Instead she is left dumbly nodding along in a boat, waiting for the boy to fall for her. It is her obsession with Eric that coerces her to mutely nod along to the song, because if he would *just kiss the girl*, then she would have all that she has wanted. It does not matter to her that she cannot verbalize anything, because she is so enamored with him and the life he represents that she seemingly abandons all aspects of her previous life. As Sells states, "Like so many women who enter 'the workforce' or any other 'male sphere,' Ariel wrestles with the double-binding cultural expectations of choosing between either voice or access, but never both" (Sells 1995:179). This statement is ratified by the depiction of Ariel embarrassedly placing her fork down after raking it through her hair as she sits in a fancy pink dress at a long dining table; she has access to the world she has always wanted, but at the cost of not being able to explain or even exhibit her innate quirkiness that was so present before. She is the outsider in a man's world, and for aspiring to be *part of that world*, she must make the ultimate sacrifice, which is not just her voice, but her identity. It is no coincidence that Ursula sings of her as a "poor, unfortunate soul" because the sea-witch is aware of something that Ariel is not: In this universe, there is no way to have both the guy and her autonomy. Or at least that is what Disney would have the audience believe. And this is the core fault of the film, especially because the audience is primarily composed of young girls. Sells describes *The Little Mermaid* as "the first in a spate of new animated features that reaffirm Disney's position as one of the largest producers of 'acceptable' role models for young girls" (Sells 1995:176). Acceptable? In a film that purports to embolden the idea of "girl power" for an audience of young girls, how is Ariel to be a role model? If Ariel is supposed to be turning her fantasy into a reality, what is the young girl's fantasy supposed to be? In a world of pretend, the film is displaying the very real and present power of patriarchy, and the "role model" is simply acquiescing to it in order to gain her prince—which is suggesting to the young female viewers that by releasing control, they will be rewarded by a happily ever after. It is here, at the close of both films, that parallels and differences reveal *The Piano* to be a feminist film, while *The Little Mermaid* is clearly conforming to the patriarchy.

The Silence of Happily-Ever-After

The closing scenes of both films offer much to interpret. *The Piano* notably offers not one, but arguably three endings within the final moments of the film. First, Ada's final act of defiance in an attempted suicide illustrates her commitment to herself. She is willing to go down with her voice, and while her foot is bound by rope, her soul is not going to be bound by patriarchal rules. Still, she changes her mind in a moment of self-actualization in which she realizes that there is more to herself than just her personal strength in regard to men. Because she truly does love Baines, she is willing to sacrifice a little for something that she desires. This is a familiar trend that is shown in *The Little Mermaid*, yet the difference is that Ada still maintains autonomy while allowing herself the pleasure that the love of another man brings her. The second "ending" shows the traditional "happily ever after," her living happily in a home with Baines, daughter Flora twirling in the grass, and a veil seen over Ada's face as she practices her verbal speech. As her fingers glide over a new piano, we see that this happy ending is not a loss. She has not given herself away, because her voice is still expressed through her music, and she still has control over herself; she has merely chosen to follow her desires. The cold metal of her fashioned-finger presses dully on the piano keys, suggesting that she has not forgotten her past, yet she is refusing to be defined by it. She is not restricted by her previous self, and she chooses to grow. Her decision to speak is crucial, as she is not forfeiting power by choosing a different form of communication; she is not forced by anyone to change, rather the change comes within herself. While silence will always be a part of her, as will her autonomy, it is no crime for her to pursue her happily ever after. Appropriately, the third and final ending of the film reveals the darker idea that she still mourns part of her soul that she has left in the ocean. It adds a bitter sense of reality to the film's end in which everything is not happy after all. Still, this can be interpreted to mean that while she has sacrificed a bit of her, she has chosen life, and she is allowed to have reminders of her past but also embrace her future. This lack of a clear answer solidifies *The Piano* as a feminist film because it offers differing perspectives on love as a determinant of happiness and a fully realized female character.

Similarly, *The Little Mermaid* concludes with the Disney traditional happily-ever-after. The evil woman is defeated, which is problematic, yet again due to the fact that Ursula is the most self-aware character in the film, and a lavish celebration ensues. The viewer is treated to a beauteous picture of Ariel and Eric's marriage ceremony on a boat, surrounded by mer-people gazing on fondly, complete with a rainbow in the sky. This over-the-top spectacle highlights the issue at hand: young women watching this film who are inadvertently lusting after this happily-ever-after, too young to consider the consequences. We see the patriarchal tradition of a father giving her daughter away in marriage, Triton acquiescing to put Ariel in the hands of a young man, as the redhead is all smiles. Yet again this is illustrating the lack of control in her life: Her decisions are always dictated by men in some degree, and she is happily willing to be bound by patriarchal society. Rather than a conclusion of Ariel merely exploring this world she so desperately wished to explore, perhaps with Eric, she is shown rushing into a marriage at the tender age of sixteen with a man she barely knows. In comparison to *The Piano*, no multiple levels or interpretations are offered to the finale of *The Little*

Mermaid, just a tidy ending for the young viewers to absorb. Here young females are told the "happy" truth: sacrifice yourself, your voice, your control—to patriarchy—and you'll be rewarded with a handsome prince and rainbows in the sky. And they all lived, happily ever after . . .

Does a film commit an unacceptable offense if it should end in happily ever after? No, of course not. There is certainly nothing fundamentally wrong with a happy ending, as a film can conclude as such and still be considered feminist. *The Piano* is a clear example of this, in which Ada is allowed the luxury of being happy while remaining true to herself. The latter part of this statement is what qualifies it to be a feminist film, the focus on the individuality of a woman, and the autonomy she displays. Silence is her tool to fight against patriarchy and to preserve her control, and she is permitted the ability to evolve. Yet, the same cannot be said about Ariel in *The Little Mermaid*. She does receive her happily ever after, yet it is at a grave cost—herself. Her silence represents her loss of control, or her willingness to bow down to patriarchal constrictions. She does not "evolve," rather she regresses from a woman who thirsts for knowledge and adventure to a timid girl awaiting a kiss in a boat. As Sells writes, "It is not simply that Ariel gives me hope, but that I have to find hope in her" (Sells 1995:186). She is not wrong; hope is desperately needed here. We need to hope that some-day Ariel will evolve into a character more like Ada, that silence will be used to empower women rather than oppress them, and that the happily ever after will not come at the cost of one's autonomy.

Works Cited

Davis, Kimberly Chabot. *Postmodern Texts and Emotional Audiences*. West Lafayette, IN: Purdue UP, 2007. Print.

Sells, Laura. "Where Do the Mermaids Stand?" *From Mouse to Mermaid: The Politics of Film, Gender, + Culture*. Ed. Elizabeth Bell, Lynda Haas, and Laura Sells. Bloomington: Indiana UP, 1995. 175–192. Print.

Annie Smith

Fish Food

2013 Honorable Mention for Excellence in Second-Year Seminar Writing

Anyone who has caught dinner on the end of a fishing rod knows that however many times he/she go out on the water, there are only a fraction of occasions when the catch is of either sufficient size or number to keep for a family meal. I've fished with my father in the warm, shallow waters of Lucas Shoals between Martha's Vineyard and the Elizabethan Islands each summer. There, we would drift for hours in silence while the gentle current carried our boat over the ocean floor where fluke congregate to feed. I can vividly remember two trips that landed three full-grown, comically disfigured fluke on our plates. On a typical trip, we'd hook one or two young fluke too small for fibbing about the size and, consequently, tossing into the cooler for transport home. Or, we'd feel nibbles on the line after drifting along the length of the Shoals, but not actually hook the creature. Very, very rarely did we reel in any keepers. Usually, the fish on our plate after our long day attempting to hit the aquatic lottery was commercially caught—we'd swing by the grocery store on our way home from the marina. Dad and I tried to pass off the fish as our own one of those times, but Mom wasn't fooled. She teased us for the rest of the week about our ineptness. While we never sustained our diets with fluke that Dad would filet on our boat, we still went fishing every summer.

Many other people fish for dinner like my father and I. Many others make their living by culling the great aquatic predators from the deep. And many more fish for recreational purposes. This treatment of fish is not wholly unjustified, according to the Judeo-Christian belief system, which dominates Western society's conceptualization of nature and humans' place in the natural world. Aldo Leopold, essayist on conservation, connects our species' tendency to subjugate the other species of the planet to our "Abrahamic concept of land," wherein humans hold dominion over all animals (Leopold 1970:xviii). Leopold further states that "We abuse land because we regard it as a commodity belonging to us" (Leopold 1970:xviii). Just as our species believes that God grants us ownership of the land, so we believe that God grants us ownership of the sea. By isolating itself in the taxonomic structure, our species has elevated humankind over all other animals.

If fish are our economic goods, then it is within our rights to harvest them. Research reveals that international waters are overfished and have been for some time. The human tradition for fishing has been long, and the worldwide consumption of fish was 86 million tons in 1998

(Allan and Tidwell 2001:958). Their 1999 EMBO Report, "Fish as Food: Aquaculture's Contribution," anticipated an increase of fish consumption to 110 million tons in 2010 (Allan and Tidwell 2001:958). These statistics are frightening to Allan and Tidwell, who interpret the increase as the result of changing first world tastes and the need for the "nutritional and financial health of a large segment of the world's population" (Allan and Tidwell 2001:958–959). They paint a horrifying portrait of the modern commercial fishing industry, which is driven by the consumer tastes:

> In the period 1990–1997, fish consumption increased 31% while the supply from marine capture fisheries increased by only 9%. This has intensified the pressure on the harvesters, which has translated into increased pressures on, and over-fishing of, many commercial fisheries. Nearly half of the known ocean fisheries are completely exploited, and 70% are in need of urgent management (Allan and Tidwell 2001:958).

The call to arms is clear. While humans once fished responsibly, the demands of the market are driving the fisheries to total depletion at an astonishing rate. Joe Roman identifies this problem in "We Shall Eat Them on the Beaches," wherein he says "We have already managed to eat several species into oblivion over the years—including the great auk and the passenger pigeon—and are having a similar effect on the world's fish stocks" (Roman 2005:41). For him as well as Allan and Tidwell, there is a need to act. Yet, the depletion of the fishing stocks is not solely the fault of the fishermen who are only trying to fill the hold, corner the market, and bring home a large paycheck; it is, in part, the fault of the human culture's voracious appetites and desire to economize food consumption. Our species has lost the concept of what it means to sacrifice an animal's life in order to preserve our own.

In ancient cultures, hunting was an act wherein a human took another creature's life with the sanction of God. To that effect, the hunter "looked the animal in the eye," a concept that Michael Pollan discusses in his book, *The Omnivore's Dilemma: A Natural History of Four Meals* (2006). He explains that these hunters also had an understanding of their actions, as evidenced by his statement: "In biblical times the rules governing ritual slaughter stipulated a rotation, so that no individual would have to kill animals every day, lest he become dulled to the gravity of the act" (Pollan 2006:331). Rituals like these were what allowed ancient humans to find solace in committing violent acts against the natural world (Pollan 2006:331). But, the commercial nature of today's fishing industry—which puts several middlemen between the consumer and the hunter—prevents the consumer from paying the captured fish the respect which it is due. It is this distance that allows humans to be blind to the horrors of commercial fishing that includes " . . . fish lost to spoilage, undetected mortality under the surface, and ghost fishing through lost equipment that continues to catch fish" (Allan and Tidwell 2001:959).

Consumers at the fish market are not generally aware that for every fish they purchase, there is another that did not reach final sale. Instead, the by-catch is forgotten.

When I fish with my father, we treasure the by-catch. Nearly all fish that grace our deck return to their watery world as soon as my father can wrest the hook from their mouths and jaws. Even after the by-catch are hundreds of feet beneath us, the stories of their cunning and fight remain with us as we head home with a fish market purchase in our truck.

Works Cited

Allan, Geoff, and James Tidwell. "Fish as Food: Aquaculture's Contribution." *EMBO Reports* 2.11 (2001): 958–963. Web. 24 March. 2013.

Leopold, Aldo. "Foreword to Sand County Almanac." Foreword. *A Sand County Almanac: With Essays on Conservation from Round River*. New York: Ballantine, 1970. Xvii–xix. Print.

Pollan, Michael. "The Ethics of Eating Animals." *The Omnivore's Dilemma: A Natural History of Four Meals*. New York: Penguin, 2006. 304–333. Print.

Roman, Joe. "We shall eat them on the beaches: we've a talent for eating species to extinction, so why not put it to good use for a change." *New Scientist* 187.2516 (2005): 41. *Academic OneFile*. Web. 24 Mar. 2013.

Thomas Scanlan Jr.

Jane Eyre and *Dr. Jekyll and Mr. Hyde:*
Defense Mechanisms in the Texts

2010 Award for Excellence in Second Year Seminar Writing

In this essay, the writer compares two novels not often brought into close juxta-position. Using a single secondary source as his starting point, the writer casts the two novelists as foreshadowing the 20th century's understanding of psychology. The writer's style is particularly dense, with many instances of complex and compound-complex sentences. Take a close look at how this writer weaves direct quotations into the essay: notice how each quotation is accompanied with an explanation of how the quotation relates to the writer's main points.

What one might not be inclined to do often, but should, is to juxtapose the works of Robert Louis Stevenson and Charlotte Bronte, mainly *Jane Eyre* with *Dr. Jekyll and Mr. Hyde.* For both of these writers show keen foresight into the field of psychology and into Sigmund Freud's prized invention, psychoanalysis. Despite predating him, both display understandings of what would come to be known as Freud's ego and id, as well as the defense mechanism of projection. Through this comprehension of the human psyche, both writers are able to display their characters' ability to detach and project undesirable aspects of their personality onto various other elements, as well as their self-conscious introjections.

One might first look at Bronte's *Jane Eyre*, where projection is being employed at several different levels. One of Sandra M. Gilbert and Susan Gubar's recurring theses is that Bertha Mason is "Jane's truest and darkest double," a constantly reappearing manifestation of Jane's suppressed feelings (360). While this is very much the case throughout the novel, the misstep one might feel they are committing in their analysis is that of allowing Bronte's consciousness while crafting this work to vanish, as well as treating Bertha Mason as a similarly invisible apparition. Clearly such a supernaturally-charged novel should be analyzed "between the lines," but while Bertha does carry out several of Jane's hidden desires, the reader, unlike any persons in the novel have done, must acknowledge Bertha Mason as a real person. So, while Gilbert and Gubar may insist that Bertha represents Jane's id and Jane simply represents her own ego, can one not argue that both justly have both an id and an ego, and that though it can be read into that Bertha carries out actions Jane subconsciously wishes for, that Bertha is, in fact, carrying out her *own conscious* wishes?

One recalls the ambiguity of Rochester's reasons for imprisoning Bertha; could this not be an example of Rochester projecting? When Jane tells Rochester that she believes he would hate her were she to become mad, he denies it adamantly. He cries, "you are mistaken. . . . *Your* mind is my treasure, and if it were broken, it would be my treasure still: if *you* raved, my arms should confine you, and not a strait waistcoat. . . . if *you* flew at me as wildly as that woman did this morning, I should receive you in an embrace" [emphasis added] (*Jane Eyre*, 301). So then, simply because he did not love Bertha as much as he apparently loves Jane at this point, Bertha is locked in an attic for fifteen years. One might look at this more closely in the novel, seeing Rochester's initial aversion to the process of arranged marriage, being "sent out to Jamaica, to espouse a bride already courted for me," after college (305). He admits that at first he was intoxicated with the exoticness of Bertha, but he then complains of how he was deceived and did not adequately know her as a person. He previously had recalled how Bertha stemmed from "three generations" of "idiots and maniacs" (292). He claims "her mother, the Creole, was both a mad woman and a drunkard!" (292). The way he treats Bertha could be interpreted as animosity towards the one he blames for his foolish, youthful mistake. When he learns that Bertha's mother was in an insane asylum, he projects the same caricature on her. Looking at his argument against her, one could easily come to the conclusion that her "intemperate and unchaste" behavior or her "giant propensities" are simply an open-mindedness toward, and yearning for, sexual stimulation that she would find perfectly reasonable, having been raised in the more indulgent atmosphere of the Caribbean, as opposed to Rochester, coming from a conservative English background, to whom such behaviors would be an affront (306). There are even undertones of racism one can detect, for example in the way Rochester needlessly refers to Bertha's mother as "the Creole," and then how he melodramatically recalls his suicide attempt halted by "a wind fresh from Europe" that "blew over the ocean" to necessitate his epiphany (308). Instead of simply deserting Bertha in Jamaica and returning home himself, his imperialistic, English subconscious tells him "you may take the maniac with you to England; confine her" (308). Thus, her subsequent breakdown is not one of insanity, perhaps, but the result of a mutual culture shock–not only was she matched with a man she shares nothing in common with; she was pigeonholed as irrevocably insane and forced to emigrate. The following fifteen years of isolation is what had turned her into the savage she is considered in the novel's present.

However, in this respect, one might argue Bertha is Jane's "truest" double. That is, they were both pigeonholed. From her earliest recollections Jane was considered a mutt of society. After the death of her uncle, her only relative (known at that time) capable of feeling love toward her, she suffered unpardonable torment at the hands of her aunt, Mrs. Reed. Her inferiority complex formed from this is staggering, a complex that remains with her until perhaps the last tender moments of the novel set in Ferndean. Thus, Jane internalizes within herself a number of rather crippling issues stemming from this complex, as well as introjecting class issues of Rochester.

These concerns are raised by Gilbert and Gubar when they attempt to psychoanalyze the dreams Jane has—though Bronte must be credited for not only understanding, but creating the implications of Jane's dreams. They see the wailing child in all the dreams as an embodiment of Jane's inability to disassociate the present Jane with her "orphan child" complex (358). They rightly claim that this is what inhibits Jane from embracing the idea of an unequal marriage, appended to the already burdensome Victorian social conventions. They go further, connecting the two women by asserting that Bertha is "the ferocious secret self Jane has been trying to repress ever since her days at Gateshead" (360). While this may certainly be the case, one could argue the case for another connection.

Despite both women's lack of opportunity in their lives, Jane does have the advantage of one crucial opportunity. She is allowed to embark on an odyssey of self-discovery, unlike Bertha Mason, who is allowed only to wither away in a cramped attic. One could argue that the most important aspect of Jane's odyssey is her interaction with her cousin St. John. This is where she is able to overcome, at least partially, the inferiority complex she has had projected onto her by herself and others and discover who she really is, which she does by overcoming the "ice," a one-word metaphor for unhappiness and passion-suppression used throughout the entire novel.

Gilbert and Gubar introduce this concept, stating "where Rochester represents the fire of her nature, her cousin represents the ice" (366). They go further, saying "while for some women ice may 'suffice,' for Jane, who has struggled all her life, like a sane version of Bertha, against the polar cold of a loveless world, it clearly will not" (366). There is great irony and injustice here. While this is a great conceptualization on their part, as feminists do they not see that Rochester should be charged for extinguishing the flame of Bertha Mason, or how unfair it is that Jane is granted the chance to reject this life of "ice," (inasmuch as she has the liberty of denying St. John's proposal, unlike Bertha, to whom incarceration is the only option)? It is, however, in a sense euthanasia on the part of Bronte to allow Bertha Mason an honorable and retributive death in burning down her prison and permanently injuring her captor at the same time Jane is allowed the opportunity she was not. In doing so, Bertha provides Jane with one more favor. In blinding and crippling Rochester, Bertha provided him and Jane with equality, something necessary for Jane to overcome her inferiority complex and the brutal class distinctions she had projected onto their romance. Only with Rochester as less of a man can Jane accept their compatibility.

The theme of the confining nature of social conventions is also to be found within Stevenson's novella, if one were drawing comparisons. It clearly precipitates much of the action in *Jane Eyre*, and is perhaps an antagonist itself equivalently in *Dr. Jekyll and Mr. Hyde* (*DJMH*). In Jekyll's account of the case it is learned that, despite the nature of his work and his generally stoic reputation, Jekyll labored his whole life to suppress his "disposition" of "a certain impatient gaiety . . . such as [he] found it hard to reconcile with my imperious desire to carry my head high, and wear a more than commonly grave countenance before the public" (103). It is evident that the character restraints that stereotyped doctors at this time have found yet another victim with Jekyll. It is so severe that when Jekyll had reached his "years of reflection," he finds himself so regretful of how he spent his time he deems it a "profound duplicity of life" that he hides with a "morbid sense of shame" (103).

There are also a number of contemporaneous sociological and historical concerns of Robert Louis Stevenson that show through the pages of the book. When Jekyll renders his version of a utopia in which mankind would be rid of the restlessness caused by the struggles of their dual natures, he says:

> If each, I told myself, could be housed in separate identities, life would be relieved of all that was unbearable; the unjust might go his way, delivered from the aspirations and remorse of his more upright twin; and the just could walk steadfastly and securely on his upward path, doing the good things in which he found his pleasure, and no longer exposed to disgrace and penitence by the hands of this extraneous evil (105).

From these lines, and many others throughout Jekyll's dissertation, one may sense some hostility toward the church, and the overwhelmingly controlling nature of Christianity, perhaps the guiltiest perpetrator of projecting in history. One could argue that this is a cleverly allegorical, satirical scolding of what Christianity and society (not clearly distinct in the historical context of *DJMH*) had done to man up to this point. Essentially Stevenson, through Jekyll as narrator, is saying that no matter how hard men try, they can never escape the "evil"—a very subjective concept itself–of their natures, and that it is foolish to think otherwise. Though not evidenced in the novel, one might say that Jekyll's creation of Hyde, or in other words, his achieving the necessary distinction of man's natures, is the only way to accomplish the impossible task of reforming man enough for salvation, a task Christianity vehemently insists is possible without this process. It also plays on the idea of *the* creation: Jekyll has projected and physically manifested Hyde from himself, initiating the necessary separation, thus being the successful creation, something perhaps Jekyll and Stevenson believe God with his omnipotent wisdom should have done when he had his chance. Yet, it must be noted that this argument does not find precedent in blaming Christianity for precipitating Jekyll's need to find an outlet for his troubles. What one may do, however, is treat the novella's symbolism.

What is also interesting in terms of projection in *DJMH*, is how people feel about Hyde, especially his image. The descriptions of Hyde rendered by various characters relate strongly to the idea of the subjectivity of evil, more specifically, how evil is one of the many Christian dogmas and was thrust upon any whom came in contact with Great Britain. During the incident with the trampling of the little girl, Mr. Enfield describes the scene with the angry mob and Hyde, "the man in the middle, with a kind of black, sneering coolness—frightened too, I could see that—but carrying it off, sir, really like Satan" (41). It is then intriguing to listen to Enfield after Utterson asks him to describe Hyde's appearance:

> He is not easy to describe. There is something wrong with his appearance; something displeasing, something down-right detestable. I never saw a man I so disliked, and yet I hardly know why (43).

Similarly uncertain and vague descriptions of Hyde are repeated throughout the novel. One could make the case, since Hyde later is learned to be the embodiment of man's amoral, evil nature, that Hyde is a statement against what evil actually is. People who see Hyde know that they should dislike him, but it is more of a tentative prejudice, like Christians dealing with right and wrong, a feeling they really cannot explain when asked—essentially what they are saying is that they know they should be against whatever evil is, but they are not sure what it is, or why they should hate it. If not for Christianity, or its predecessor Judaism, the western world would be at a loss over what evil or wrong was (not that they helped much regardless), a concept acknowledged here by Stevenson in this allegorical scene. The main point here is that the church has imposed two oppressive forces on mankind: one, they provide the basis for social conventions and pressures that drive men to the extremes in which their evil natures are awakened and manifested; and two, the belief that these new behaviors are unnatural, sins that need to be repented for lest one goes to "hell." Stevenson has shown that the church set the parameters for what this evil nature would be, while simultaneously causing mankind to the very boundaries and subsequently to the foggy exteriors of those same parameters.

At very basic levels, both *Jane Eyre* and *DJMH* are about characters constantly at battle with social conventions and self-image. These themes meld into the infinitely larger theme of human restlessness, the struggle most of the populations in the world's history have experienced and have found no worthy answer for. So while both of these works show almost prophetic insight into psychology and how human nature is understood today, equally as wise, they depict an understanding that humans, based on their natures, have virtually no foreseeable hope of discovering how to cope harmoniously with the world they live in, at least not until someone finds the solution. And of course there is always hope for that.

Works Cited

Bronte, Charlotte. *Jane Eyre*. Oxford World's Classics ed. New York City: Oxford University Press, 2000. Print.

Gilbert, Sandra M., and Susan Gubar. *The Madwoman in the Attic: The Woman Writer and the Nineteenth-Century Literary Imagination*. New Haven And London: Yale University Press, 1979. 358–69. Print.

Stevenson, Robert L. *Dr. Jekyll and Mr. Hyde*. Signet Classic ed. New York City: Penguin Books, 2003. Print.

Gregory Alcaro

Immanuel Kant's Moral Philosophy

2009 Award Winner for Excellence in Second Year Seminar Writing

This essay which challenges aspects of Kant's moral philosophy has many of the features of an effectively written argument: a clearly stated thesis, clear forecasting in the first paragraph of what will follow in the rest of the essay, and carefully laid out claims with thoughtful interpretations of Kant's work as evidence and concrete examples. Toward the end of the essay, the writer considers a counterargument, and then deftly returns to his own position—a move often made in writing in philosophy. In your view, how else does this essay "sound" like a philosophy paper? What moves made in this essay would be equally effective in essays written for other disciplines? What differences have you noticed in the ways that writers in different disciplines argue?

Morality is one basis in society that helps to determine if one's actions or motives are right or wrong. Philosopher Immanuel Kant, in 1785, presented the notion of the categorical imperative that he believed determined and instituted the greatest principal of morality. In this paper, I will argue that although the categorical imperative comes close to determining the supreme principal of morality, it falls short in that it fails to recognize consequences as an important aspect for universal moral decisions. I will show the flaws of Kant's moral philosophy by presenting and discussing the categorical imperative, Kant's definition of morality as well as the universalism of morals, and challenge Kant's notion that consequences are irrelevant.

The categorical imperative as Kant would say, "is not concerned with the matter of the action and its intended result, but rather with the form of the action and the principle from which it follows; what is essentially good in the action consists in the mental disposition, let the consequences be what they may" (p. 26, 416). Here, Kant is stating that consequences are irrelevant and one must not use another person or anything at all as a means to an end. Furthermore, what he is really saying is that action in itself is what is relevant. In addition, according to Kant, knowledge of moral laws is "a priori" (p. 29, 420), which means that for one to gain a universal depiction of moral laws they must not rely on experience. To elaborate further, morals cannot be gained through experience, but rather are naturally inherent in our nature. The universal formulation of the categorical imperative must be then used to determine the morality of an action. Kant, in his words, states this formulation as "I should never act except in such a way that I can also will that my maxim should become a universal law" (p. 14, 402). In this quote, Kant is stating that one should never commit an act, unless their personal desire behind their action can be willed into a universal moral law.

The universal formulation of the categorical imperative consists of four steps to determine morality. First, one must formulate their maxim, or, in other words, establish one's personal desire or subjective inclination behind one's action. Second, one must then universalize their maxim in the sense that one treats all of humanity as acting upon that particular desire or inclination. In other words, we assume every person follows that maxim as a universal moral law. Third, one must subject this universal law to a logical test. That is, can this maxim be universalized without lapsing into a logical contradiction? If not, then the action behind the maxim is deemed immoral. If so, then one proceeds to the fourth step. Fourth, upon passing the third step, one must subject this law to a further test. Here, one imagines if they can *rationally* will their maxim into a universal law that all should follow as basis for morality. If not, then the action becomes immoral. If, however, the maxim passes this test, we can say that the action is morally acceptable. We must now apply the categorical imperative to an action and determine its morality.

Kant states, "the man who contemplates suicide will ask himself whether his action can be consistent with the idea of humanity as an end in itself (p. 36, 429). Inevitably, the act of suicide, for Kant, is an immoral act and goes against the categorical imperative. This is determined through the universal formulation. First, the maxim of suicide would be "I want to kill myself because I love myself." Second, now let's universalize this maxim and say that "everyone kills themselves out of self-love." Third, the maxim must be logically tested and the results would be that human life is over, leading to a logical contradiction—the love of life contradicting the end of life. The maxim of suicide makes it impossible to reach step four because of the logical contradiction that occurs and therefore suicide is immoral. This not only concludes that suicide is immoral, but it also violates the categorical imperative and the notion that all have a perfect duty not to kill themselves.

It must now be presented Kant's argument that the categorical imperative rather than "rules of skill" (p. 26, 416) is what we ought to use to determine what is moral. Kant argues this by first stating that "For law alone involves the concept of a necessity that is unconditioned and indeed objective and hence universally valid, and commands our laws which must be obeyed, i.e. must be followed even in opposition to inclination" (p. 26, 416). In this quote, Kant is stating that we have a set of universal moral laws that are naturally inherent which we must abide by regardless of the doubt we may have in them. Kant also supports his categorical imperative by stating, "on the other hand, the categorical imperative is limited by no condition, and can quite properly be called a command since it is absolutely, though practically, necessary" (p. 26, 416). Here, Kant explains that the categorical imperative has no limitations upon it when it is used to determine the morality of an action and also that one must live by this imperative because it is an absolute necessity to life. Kant argues how the categorical imperative is consistent with his understanding of morality.

Kant's argument that proves the categorical imperative to be consistent with his standards of morality can be broken down into five simple logical steps. First, Kant has a set of criteria that moral rules must meet to be in fact moral. The criteria that Kant has set are that consequences and contexts are irrelevant to the moral evaluation of our actions, only motivation counts, knowledge of moral laws is a priori (that is, known independent of experience), the laws are universal, and they are normative (that is, they tell us what we "ought" to do). Second, there are only two categories of imperatives which are the hypothetical (i.e., rules and skill, and counsels of prudence) and categorical (p. 26, 416). A hypothetical imperative unlike the categorical allows one to take actions which bring about happiness for the individual. Also, consequences are relevant and all knowledge is a posteriori (i.e., known through experience) unlike the categorical. Third, the hypothetical imperative fails to meet some of the criteria that Kant has set. It fails to be consistent because consequences are considered irrelevant and all knowledge is a priori. Fourth, the categorical imperative however meets all the criteria. Fifth, Kant concludes that the categorical imperative is the imperative to use for determining moral laws. Therefore, through these five logical steps it can be concluded for Kant that his notion of the categorical imperative is consistent with his understanding of morality and that all should use this imperative when determining moral laws as opposed to the hypothetical.

While I agree with Kant's claim that morals should be held universally, I argue that Kant is wrong in the sense that consequences are irrelevant; rather I maintain that they are an important aspect for universal moral decisions. I hold this position because in life one may be put into a situation where they must lie because they considered the consequences if they did not lie and those consequences would be horrific. This situation can be explained through the example commonly referred to as "the axe-wielding murderer."

Let's suppose a man has gone crazy with an axe trying to kill a person you know you're in the same house with. This man running with the axe then runs into you. The man then asks you where your friend is. Lo and behold, you know that your friend is hiding upstairs. Now, right here Kant would say that we all have a duty not to lie and one must always be honest. So, in this case Kant would say we are morally obligated to tell "this axe-wielding murderer" trying to kill your friend where he is. This is where I maintain that consequences are relevant because the universal moral decision in this situation, I hold, would be to not tell the man where your friend is in order to save your friend's life.

In this objection, I am challenging Kant's criteria of moral evaluation, which he assumes in the first premise of his argument that the categorical imperative is the proper moral law. Here, I maintain, that Kant is mistaken in his first premise when he states that consequences are irrelevant. I am suggesting that there are situations in life where the consequences are relevant and significant to the moral evaluation of actions. Therefore, since consequences are relevant, Kant's argument that justifies the categorical imperative loses part of its grounding since the categorical imperative does not take consequences into account.

A Kantian would now object to my position by arguing that the counter-example provided mistakenly encapsulates the response to the individual who wishes to uphold one's duty to protect one's friend. More specifically, the Kantian would maintain that the consequences are still irrelevant, as one can still be honest and protect a friend's well-being. Kant would support this notion by arguing that one would not be lying or contributing to their friend's death by stating, "I know where my friend went, but I will not tell you." Kant would maintain from this statement that the categorical imperative remains the proper way to determine moral laws. As such, consequences are still irrelevant.

Even though the Kantian, in this case, has a made a logical objection, they are still wrong in saying that consequences are irrelevant and to never lie. This can be argued by pointing out that Kant's statement to the axe-wielding murderer ("I know where my friend went, but I will not tell you"), not only puts one's friend's life at risk still but, one's life as well. It can put one's life at risk because the "but I will not tell you" clause could be taken as hostility or antagonism by this axe-wielding murderer, in turn leading to one's own death. But, since we have a moral obligation to avoid our own deaths, it follows that this Kantian response would not work. Once again, the consequences in this situation suggest to us that the right thing to do is lie to the axe-wielding murderer. Hence, I maintain that consequences are always relevant and the right thing to do still is to lie for the sake of one's friend's life, as well as their own.

Thus, I could never agree with Kant's claims that it is universally moral to not consider the consequences. In addition, if anyone had not considered the consequences in this situation, they would have contributed to their friend's death, or their own, and I for one hold that to be immoral.

I conclude that, though the categorical imperative comes close to determining the supreme principal of morality, it falls short in that it fails to recognize consequences as an important aspect for universal moral decisions. Thus, without consequences it would be nearly impossible for one to ever establish a strict set or moral decisions.

Works Cited

Kant, Immanuel. *Grounding for the Metaphysics of Morals 3rd ed.* Trans. James W. Ellington, Indianapolis: Hackett Publishing Company, Inc, 1993. 14–36.

Writing on the Topic of Sustainability

Michael Faherty

And the Winner Is . . .

2009 Award for Excellence in Writing on the Topic of Sustainability

In this essay, the author addresses the three key areas of sustainability: environment, economy, and social justice. Using data which appears accurate and well-referenced he makes a strong argument. This author, like some of the others in this text, uses a framing device for his essay, which introduces the concept of learning from those who come before us. The author's final line returns to this frame to warn that those truly interested in sustainability should look to what others have been doing.

***

Boast not against the branches. But if thou boast, thou bearest not the root, but the root thee (Romans 11:18, KJV).

Last Sunday, the 81st Annual Academy Awards kicked off at the Kodak Theatre in Los Angeles, California. Although the spotlight was on the nominees, the acceptance speeches were not. All Oscar recipients were aware that their achievements are owed to someone else's support and sacrifice along the way. Their gratitude extended to family members, friends, co-workers, and fans. The winner, or "branch," realized he or she could not have thrived without the nourishment of the "root."

Less can be said about America's achievements as a country. Had it not been for Native Americans, the early settlers from Europe would not have survived on the newly discovered soil. Even today, our country, along with other industrialized nations, exploits Indigenous peoples around the world for their knowledge. Omitting Indigenous peoples from our acceptance speech would show how far our "branch" has grown from the "root." We have ignored the nourishment of our ancestors, and relied on unsustainable nutrients such as fossil fuels. In addition to knowledge of the land, Indigenous peoples have contributed much more to modern society. Their survival skills also dwell in their spiritual relationship with the land, ability to manage resources, and their holistic approach to social relations. If modern societies intend to subsist in the future, they must look back to their roots, and rediscover their inseparable connection to nature.

The Cree Indians of Canada embody a lifestyle worthy of emulating across the globe. Their sustainable lifestyle has enabled them to survive harsh North American climates for over 3,000 years (Richardson, Ianzelo, & Low, 1974). Cree Indians have identified approximately 400 species of medicinal plants, with over 2,000 applications (Johns et al., 2007). The most familiar plant is the Acorus Calamus. It has functioned as an alleviator for toothaches, fatigue, diabetes, and bowel pains (Cesspooch, 2005). Natural alternatives for alleviating illness would certainly help the financial burden prescription drugs place on many Americans today. Instead of making medicine free for all, companies have turned the drug industry into a lucrative business. *Fortune Magazine* ranks pharmaceutical companies as the most profitable business in the United States (Moser, 2002).

Nothing is more sacred to the Cree Indians than the land. It nourishes, teaches, and supports the people's way of life. Sam Blacksmith, a Cree Indian leader in the Mistassini group, states what it is like hunting on his territory:

> *A man who lives by hunting cherishes the land. He cherishes his way of life. Appreciates what he gets from the land. A man will still go to the land when life is hard. This is the man who truly respects the land (Richardson et al., 1974).*

The Cree Indians also encompass a spiritual respect for the animals sharing the land. Rituals are performed during the "killing, eating, and caring for the bones of the animals" (Richardson et al., 1974). According to the Cree Indian, the bear is the most revered animal of the land. Respecting the bear in its natural habitat is believed to help the hunters kill the large animal. In the event of an imbalance in nature, the Cree Indians often use a ceremony to reestablish harmony. While hunting one day for large game, Cree hunters killed a pregnant female moose. The unfortunate discovery prompted the hunters to perform a ritual to ensure the moose population will flourish. The hunters placed a piece of the mother inside the dead calf's mouth and said, "We give a little of the life of the mother to the calf" (Richardson et al., 1974). Respect for land and wildlife was not on Quebec Premier Robert Bourassa's conscience after implementing the James Bay Hydroelectric Project in 1971. His diverting rivers into the La Grande River to help make electricity flooded approximately 11,000 sq. km. of northern forest with the excess water (Saganash, 2008). This irreversible act destroyed many hunting and sacred burial grounds.

Resource management is imperative to the survival of the Cree Indians. They are very careful not to exploit the land's resources. Each year, Cree leaders scout out their territory to measure its carrying capacity. If the area is not fertile, the leaders will look elsewhere. Mr. Blacksmith suspected his territory to be quite abundant, and invited two other families to be guests from September to June. Jolly's family territory, on the other hand, required more time to replenish its vegetation and animal population. The practice of abandoning a campsite to allow for rejuvenation of the land is a form of shifting cultivation. On the other

And the Winner Is . . .

hand, resource management for sustainability has been given little consideration in modern societies. In fact, according to estimates by the World Wildlife Fund (WWF), "three planets would be required were everyone to adopt the consumption patterns and lifestyles of the average citizen from the United Kingdom; five planets, were they to live like the average North American" (World Business Council for Sustainable Development, 2008).

Social cohesion is a tremendous asset coveted by Indigenous peoples and is often overlooked by industrialized cultures. Genders play complementary, if not equal, roles in society. The Cree men will spend weeks looking for big game, such as caribou and moose, while the women remain behind to maintain the camp. Mr. Blacksmith declares, "Everyone has a place in the scheme of daily life" (Richardson, et al., 1974). Inside the lodge, three families manage to balance community living with privacy. Although each family occupies a corner of the lodge and supplies their own food, families are willing to share if there happens to be any signs of disparity. In a country that rewards and promotes individualism, the United States is far from living a communal lifestyle. A helping hand infrequently reaches further than the nuclear family. Also, gender equality has yet to be realized. The median annual earnings for women are still 22.2% lower than their male counterpart, although it is hoped that, under the Lilly Ledbetter Fair Pay Restoration Act of 2009, there will in the future be less discrimination based on "sexual orientation or gender identity or expression" (White House, 2009). A Holistic approach to living in the United States would reduce poverty, crime, discrimination, and many other by-products created from an economic driven society.

Indigenous peoples hold the key to humanity's future. Not only are they "guardians of the extensive and fragile ecosystems," but they are models for a just society (Strong, 1990). The fruits of modern society's labor will soon diminish if it continues to pursue the present course of development. The United States can receive the Oscar for "The Most Sustainable Country" category only if we begin to recognize and learn from the origins of our success.

References

Cesspooch, L. (2005). Acorus Calamus L.: A sacred medicinal plant of the Native Cree. *Utah Department of Health: Diabetes Prevention and Control Program.* (pp. 1–2) Retrieved February 25, 2009, from http://health.utah.gov/diabetes/pdf/telehlth/cesspooch_acorus_calamusL.pdf

Johns, T., Arnason, J.T., Dugas, M., Cuerrier, A., Prentki, M., & Haddad, P. (2007). Project investigates use of medicinal plants for diabetes in Cree. *Health Canada. Science and Research.* Retrieved February 25, 2009, from http://www.hc-sc.gc.ca/sr-sr/activ/consprod/cree-cries-eng.php)

Moser, J. (2002). Links between drug company profitability and investments in research: A fact sheet. *Galen Institute.* Retrieved February 25, 2009, from http://www.multisclerosis.org/news/Jul2002/DrugCompanyProfitsvsResearch.html

Richardson, B., Ianzelo, (Producers), & Low, C. (Director). (1974). *The Cree Hunters of Mistassni* [Online Videotape]. National Film Board of Canada.

Saganash, E. (2008). Eeyou Istchee: Land of the Cree: The grand council is born. *Canadian Broadcasting Company.* Retrieved February 25, 2009, from http://archives.cbc.ca/society/native_issues/topics/2473/

Strong, M. (1990). Why is Indigenous knowledge important? *United Nations Educational, Scientific, and Cultural Organization.* Retrieved February 25, 2009, from http://www.unesco.org/education/tlsf/TLSF/theme_c/mod11/mod11task0l/mod11task01s02.htm

The White House (2009). Civil Rights: Combat employment discrimination. *The White House.* Retrieved February 25, 2009, from http://www.whitehouse.gov/agenda/civil_rights/

World Business Council for Sustainable Development—WBCSD. (2008). Sustainable Consumption Facts and Trends: From a Business Perspective. *World Business Council for Sustainable Development.* (pp. 1–40) Retrieved February 25, 2009, from http://www.wbcsd.org/DocRoot/19Xwhv7X5V8cDlHbHC3G/WBCSD_Sustainable_Consumption_web.pdf